Buddy Hull

This book
belongs to:
Evelyn Arbo

BUDDY STALL'S
BIG EASY

BUDDY STALL'S

BIG EASY

By Gaspar J. "Buddy" Stall

HARLO PRINTING

Printed by Harlo Printing Company,
50 Victor, Detroit, Michigan 48203

Dedicated To

Aunt Lena, Uncle Bill,
and their four sons, my cousins,
Jake, Steve, Billy and Paul.

Acknowledgements

Special thanks to Clyde Morrison, Julie Dawson, Roxanne Ryan, Lane Casteix, Wade and Yvette Ponthier, Irvin Bergeron, Carol and Jim Rohde, Marietta and Richard Herr, Joe d'Aquin, Kendall Stall, Judge Dick Garvey, as well as the following people: Collin Hamer and the entire staff of the Louisiana Division of the New Orleans Public Library, Pamela Arceneaux and the entire staff of the Historic New Orleans Collection.

Foreword

As a student of New Orleans' history, it didn't take long for me to realize the city's history is, without question, more entertaining than fiction. I do not believe there has ever been anyone who has had the fertile mind necessary to create things that would have been as entertaining as the history lived by the people of this city. Years of study have also convinced me that the influx of multitudes of people from various parts of the world, from the city's birth until this day, is the main reason New Orleans is the unique city that it is and always has been. The Big Easy was the "melting pot" of humanity in North America (65 different nationalities prior to the Civil War) long before New York began using the term to describe itself.

After writing six books about any city, one would think that in writing the seventh the main problem would be in finding sufficient material to fill the pages. That is not the challenge when writing about New Orleans. I found that, in writing this book, I would have the same problem as in the previous six. That is, what can or should I leave out? The information collected and written is far more than the volume requires.

Because I feel that a good sense of humor has been the single most important ingredient that helped the citizens survive the unbelievable hardships they have been required to endure, I have taken the liberty of interjecting humor where I felt it was appropriate without taking away from the historical aspect of the material.

One of my aims in writing this book is to cause you to say over and over, even though you might be a local, "I didn't know that." I also hope that the material covered will make locals proud to be citizens of this very special city, and visitors upon completing the book, have a deep desire to revisit the city, savor its charm, take part in its celebrations, indulge in its tasty foods, and, above all, rub shoulders with its number one product, its people.

CONTENTS

CHAPTER ONE

POLITICS

INTRODUCTION

To begin this chapter, let us start off with a political, historical, tongue-in-cheek story, meaning it isn't true, but it is still a good story.

George Washington, the "Father of our country", was born in Louisiana on Bayou Lafourche. When he was only four years old, his father came home one day and found little George with a broad smile on his face and one hand behind his back. Lying horizontally beside George was the old man's favorite cypress tree. Old man George called his son over to him. "What do you want, Papa?" asked young George. His father replied, "Did you cut down my favorite cypress tree?" George lifted the little hatchet he was holding behind his back, and, still smiling, said, "Father, I cannot tell a lie; I cut it down." Papa George

packed up and moved his family to Virginia, saying, "My boy will never make it in Louisiana politics."

Warranted or unwarranted, this is the opinion that people around the country have of this state's politics. The facts are, New Orleans and Louisiana have no more or no less percentage of bad politicians than any other area of the country. What we do have is a negative reputation that will take generations to change.

For one example of bad politics elsewhere, let us look back in history to the year New Orleans was founded.

STORY OF LORD CORNBURY

Just about the time New Orleans was founded, the governor of New York was Lord Cornbury. Lord Cornbury served as the governor of New York for six years. He appeared at public ceremonies in full drag, wearing a dress, silk stockings and an elaborate hairdo. He let his nails grow long and customarily donned high-heeled boots.

You will have to search long and hard to find such a story, but they do exist in almost every small, medium or large city in the country, the difference being, in New Orleans, the locals seem to accentuate the negative and eliminate the positive. If Lord Cornbury had been a New Orleans politician, everyone in the country would have known about him. In other places, when a skeleton is found in the political arena, it is put in a concrete room with a steel door and the door is welded shut. If a political skeleton in a closet is found in New Orleans, it is put in the spotlight for all to see. When this is done, we call the national media and they have a feast day at our expense.

OFFICE HOLDERS

PRIOR TO STATEHOOD

In early Louisiana, government officials acquired their offices through one of three methods:
1.   Appointment by the king.
2.   Through military rank.
3.   Outright purchase—
      positions of this nature were known as "Venal Offices".
With the amount of money spent to run for office in Louisiana today, it is possible all political offices could be considered "Venal Offices".

COLONIAL DAYS

I would like to buy:
One governorship,
One tax collector position,
One Justice of the Peace.

PRESENT DAY

I would like to buy:
150 television spots,
500 radio spots,
75 full pages of print advertising.

MAYORS OF NEW ORLEANS

When one speaks of the diversity of New Orleans, the mayors of the city do not have to take a back seat to anyone. Through the years, the city has been led by men with various ethnic backgrounds. A few examples: Etienne de Boré and Trudeau were French. Monroe, Lewis and Flower were English. Kennedy, Flanders, Fitzpatrick, and Burke represented the Irish. The Italians were represented by Maestri and Schiro. The city's two most recent mayors, Barthelemy and Morial, are African-Americans.

The city's mayors have done their share to make our political history as spicy and hot as a bottle of Tabasco. There were some who were self-taught and others who received the finest education money could buy. Some came from the social register and others from the wrong side of the tracks. There have been some related to royalty, and one a descendant of a president of the United States. Others were just common folk. Through the years, a number of them simply quit or resigned. During the Civil War, the mayor was sentenced to federal prison and was denied seeing his dying son unless he signed an oath of allegiance to the Union. Some mayors were appointed, while others had to work hard to be elected. Bob Maestri went in unopposed, while others were required to fight a political war, with military equipment being used on both sides. This chapter covers the first mayors who were appointed, as well as the first elected mayor, who did not speak, read or understand the English language. Yes, we shall learn of a city literally divided, but still able to survive. You will read of mayors who were complete opposites, but still accomplished their goals. Over the course of years, only one mayor died in office, and only one mayor became Rex, King of Mardi Gras. This chapter will also cover the unusual situation whereby, officially, New Orleans had three mayors in one day.

After you have read this chapter, I think you will agree that if you were asked you would unhesitatingly state that the mayors of the great City of New Orleans have truly added political spice to the lives of those they governed.

APPOINTED MAYORS OF NEW ORLEANS

Prior to Louisiana becoming the eighteenth state of the Union, the city's first five mayors were all appointed. They were:

Etienne de Boré - November 30, 1803, to May 26, 1804
James Pitot - June 2, 1804, to July 26, 1805
John Watkins - July 27, 1805, to March 8, 1807
James J. Mather - March 9, 1807, to May 16, 1812
Charles Trudeau - May 16, 1812, to October 8, 1812

ETIENNE DE BORÉ

Etienne de Boré, the city's first mayor, was world-renowned, not for his achievements as mayor but for being the first man in history to successfully granulate sugar commercial-

ly. De Boré's plantation ran from the river to beyond Claiborne Avenue and occupied what is now Audubon Park, Tulane and Loyola Universities and adjacent lands. In 1797, de Boré took a huge gamble by planting sugar cane on his entire plot of ground. This being a bold move never tried before, his friends told him he was flirting with disaster. No one in the world had achieved what he proposed to do. Some said no one in his right mind would attempt what de Boré proposed. Some friends even implied that de Boré might be smoking some of those funny weeds. De Boré's gamble paid off. He did what he said he would do, and in doing so, became world famous, not to mention independently wealthy.

In 1803, when Louisiana Governor William C. C. Claiborne was looking for a mayor for New Orleans, the shining star of de Boré's achievements made him a likely candidate.

Just as de Boré became world-renowned for his achievements, his grandson, Charles Gayarre, became equally distinguished in Louisiana. He became the state's first historian. His four-volume history of Louisiana is considered one of the principal works on Louisiana history.

When Tulane University built a football stadium, it was called the "Sugar Bowl". Apropos, wouldn't you say? It was on this very ground that the stadium occupied that sugar was successfully granulated commercially for the first time in history. The iron kettle in which this great achievement was performed is in Baton Rouge, on the LSU campus next to, what else, the LSU experimental sugar refinery.

MEMBER OF NOBILITY

As a young boy, Etienne was sent to France to be educated. Upon leaving school, he became one of the king's Mousquetaires or guardsmen. No one could be a Mousquetaire if he was not a member of nobility. You could say de Boré went from a prince of France to the king of the world's sugar industry.

SWEETNESS

Three short sugar-related facts that are sure to leave you with a good taste in your mouth are:

1.   New Orleanian, Josef Delarose Lascaux, was the man who invented cotton candy, the first candy to melt in your mouth, not in your hand.

2.   Pralines. The name is derived from the name of the French marshal and diplomat Ce'sar du Plessis Praslin (pronounced ''pra'lin''), later the Duke de Choisel. It

was Marshal Praslin, who, according to legend, prefer-
red his almonds cooked in sugar. Since almonds were not
readily available to early French inhabitants of Louisiana, the meat from the pecan was substituted. Presto!
The pecan praline became the most popular confection
of our area.

3.　Taste was sweet, but cost was bittersweet.
When New Orleans was very young, sugar was a costly
luxury. Its scarcity and high cost were the two major fac-
tors causing it to be used almost exclusively for medicinal
purposes.

CITY'S FIRST ELECTED MAYOR
1812

In 1812, Louisiana became the eighteenth state of the
United States. A very short time later, Orleanians were preparing to go to war against England. At the same time, they were
also preparing for their very first political war. James Pitot, one
of the earlier appointed mayors, ran against a highly successful,
extremely proud Frenchman named Nicholas Girod. Girod was
very shrewd. He convinced the voters (white male property
owners only) that Pitot, as President of New Orleans Naviga-
tional Company, had a conflict of interest. Almost all commerce at that time in history entered the city by way of Bayou
St. John and the Carondelet canal. This route was controlled by
Pitot's company. It also proved to be an albatross around

MAYOR SWORN-IN IN FRENCH!

Pitot's neck. On election day, September 21, 1812, Girod won easily, 857 to 461.

When Girod was inaugurated, the ceremonies were done in French. The reason: Girod did not speak, read or understand the English language. When Girod took office, it was suggested that since he was now mayor of an American city he should learn to speak the English language. He, in return, suggested that since he was mayor, let the people learn to speak French!

Someone jokingly said that when Girod bled he did so in red, white & blue, representing the tri colors of the French flag, not the American flag.

Nicholas Girod has the distinction of being not only the first elected mayor of New Orleans; he was also the first mayor to be re-elected.

As a staunch Frenchman and a great devotee to Napoleon, in the spring of 1821, Girod began construction of a house at 124 Chartres Street, at the corner of St. Louis. As the house was being built, Girod had what was believed to be the fastest ship in the world. Her name was "Seraphine". She was outfitted and ready to go on a secret voyage to rescue Napoleon from St.

Helena. The ship was to be captained by the famous Dominick You, one of Lafitte's capable lieutenants. Unfortunately, the Emperor died before the plot to rescue him could be carried out. The house built by Girod is still standing and has been called since it's completion, "The Napoleon House". It was here in this famous structure that Girod died on September 1, 1840, at 9:00 p.m. at the age of 90.

Girod's will proved that he was also a great philanthropist. He left one hundred thousand dollars for construction of a building to care for, what else, "French" orphans inhabiting the State of Louisiana. Charity Hospital received $30,000 and orphan asylums in New Orleans $30,000. To five of his closest friends he left $150,000. The balance of the estate, which was quite vast, went to his family.

BRAVEST MAYOR
1860 - 1862
1866 - 1867

JOHN T. MONROE

Mayor Monroe was a blood relative of U.S. President James Monroe. In spite of his impressive blood line, he arrived in New Orleans at age 20 with only $3.00 in his pocket. With little money and no contacts in a strange city, he literally started from the bottom. He began by working ordinary laboring jobs. The jobs might have been ordinary, but his diligence and efforts were not. It wasn't long before he became labor leader on the riverfront. He worked hard and mixed well with people of all classes. His perpetual drive and even temperament were just two of the many qualities he used to enter politics. His job as a labor leader taught him to fight hard for what he believed in. He was elected mayor in 1860. One of his main focuses was in the area of street railways. During his term in office he had the tracks located on Canal Street moved to the neutral ground where they remain until this day. Under his guidance, the first steam dummies replaced horse-drawn cars. This brought the suburb of Carrollton within relatively short distance of the principal part of the city.

Conditions in New Orleans were so prosperous prior to the Civil War, the term used to describe it was the Golden Era. This condition was reversed rather quickly when the war began. Within one year after the war started, the City of New Orleans fell to the invading Union forces. It was at that time that Mayor Monroe was labeled the bravest mayor in the city's history. The circumstances leading to that title were as follows:

Although New Orleans fell without a fight to the Yankee invaders, the mayor refused to lower the Confederate flag flying over City Hall or surrender the city to Admiral David Glasgow Farragut whose federal fleet lay at anchor in the harbor. After a period of prolonged correspondence between Admiral Farragut and Mayor Monroe, during which the mayor stuck to his guns in reference to hauling down the Confederate flag, Farragut became quite perturbed. On April 29, 1862, Farragut sent a detachment to remove it. All the marines in the fleet, accompanied by two large brass howitzers, made their way through the defiant crowd to City Hall. The howitzers were placed in front of City Hall facing both directions of St. Charles Street. Both howitzers were fully loaded and ready to fire.

The captain of the marines requested again the mayor lower the flag, but again Monroe refused. As the marines were sent to the roof of City Hall to remove the flag the mayor calmly walked down the stairs in front of City Hall and placed himself directly in front of one of the loaded cannons. He then simply

folded his arms and fixed his eyes on the gunner who stood ready to fire. The flag was finally removed and taken back to Admiral Farragut's ship. Mayor Monroe had not actually surrendered, but the city was nevertheless firmly in federal hands.

When General Benjamin Franklin Butler, head of the federal army occupation forces, took control of the city and found out how the mayor had defied Admiral Farragut, he sentenced Monroe to prison. He remained at Fort Pickens until the war ended. It was while he was incarcerated he suffered his greatest pain. He received a communication from Union General Butler stating that if he would take the oath of allegiance to the Union, he would be allowed to return to New Orleans to be with his dying son. Monroe, a man of deep principles, rejected the offer promptly and firmly. He never saw his son alive again.

After the war ended, Monroe returned home and was given a hero's welcome. He was nominated for mayor, elected and once again served his adopted city.

Upon retiring, he moved to Savannah, Georgia, where he lived until his death. One year later, his body was brought to New Orleans and placed in a tomb in Cypress Grove Cemetery beside the body of his son, who died while he was in prison.

Monroe was described as a man of exceptional character, a strong practical mind, dauntless courage, and unquestionable integrity. Yes, without doubt, he was the city's bravest mayor.

CHARLES M. WATERMAN
1856 - 1858

WHAT A LEGACY!

True, all mayors, because of the nature of the job, go through some turbulence during their tenures. Mayor Waterman's was a little different. Turbulence was with him his entire time in office.

Waterman was, in a sense, raised with a silver spoon in his mouth. His father was owner of the highly successful "Black Ball" steamboat line running between New York and European ports. His success allowed him to send his son to the finest schools available. Waterman used his training well. He was able to expand on the family fortune by investing in the hardware business.

Politics somehow got into his veins. He was nominated for mayor by the "Know Nothing" Party, and was elected.

CHARLES M.WATERMAN
KNOW NOTHING PARTY
CANDIDATE

His administration was disgraced from the very beginning by violence and bloodshed. The inefficiency of the city government was becoming very apparent, and after repeated riots by certain elements, Waterman simply deserted his post as mayor and took up residency near Jackson Square. There, he was visited by A. G. Brice and Judge A. G. Semmes, who endeavored to induce him to return to City Hall in order to swear in a special police force in place of the regular force. These two gentlemen urged him to do this or resign. This, they said would allow the president of the council to deal resolutely with the situation. Rather than accept this alternative, Waterman made out a paper authorizing Recorder Stith to swear in the special police force in his place.

At the next scheduled meeting of the council, it was the understanding of the members that Waterman would appear and explain his recent actions. However, he was not present when the meeting convened. Instead, he sent a message asking what protection he could expect if he decided to attend. Recorder Stith was sent to his place near Jackson Square to tell him that he would receive safe conduct to City Hall. The unruly behavior of the crowd, which had again assembled in Lafayette Square, gave cause to his fears. The mayor agreed to accompany Stith, but upon reaching the St. Charles Hotel he learned of the evil conduct of the crowd and refused to proceed any further. Having not made it to the meeting, he was impeached.

The next day when New Orleanians awoke, they learned to find that a large part of the city had passed into control of the Vigilance Committee. The city government had practically ceased to function, and Civil War, if not actually in progress, was threatening. United States Army Captain J. K. Duncan was summoned to evaluate the situation. He immediately stationed troops around Jackson Square. He also had troops occupy the

HEADQUARTERS OF THE NEW ORLEANS VIGILANCE COMMITTEE

Cabildo and posted sentinels at all approaches to the downtown area of the city. Once this was done, the Vigilance Committee of unlawful special police were dispersed and the city police once again took control until a new mayor could be elected.

Besides impeachment as a legacy, Waterman is also known as the first mayor of any American city to issue licenses for lewd and abandoned women. He sold these for $300.00 each, charging his clients an extra dollar to have the certificates notarized. When this was done, he then kept all records in his personal possession.

№ 19.

LICENSE

Mayoralty of New-Orleans

City Hall 30ᵗʰ day of _May_ 1857

Miss _May Baily_

Having paid the Tax imposed by Ordinance No. 3267 concerning Lewd and Abandoned Woman she is hereby authorized to occupy until 31ˢᵗ January, 1858 the second or other than the first floor of the building at dwelling situated on _Dauphine_ street, No. _423_ between _St. Louis_ street and _Conti_ street.

Provided the provisions of the aforesaid Ordinance in all its particulars be complied with.

Chas. M. Waterman Mayor.

We have all heard the saying never two without three. Well, besides the dubious legacy of impeachment and selling of licenses to prostitutes, Waterman still had one more item to add to his legacy. Just as his political life was in constant turmoil, he was a controversial figure to the end. He left his home one day and never was seen or heard from again. A note which he left gave cause to believe he meant to commit suicide. His hat with his initials was found on board the second district ferry boat. The levees on both sides of the river were searched by men on foot, and numerous boats were sent into the river to search for his body, but with no success.

In spite of his stormy political life, he was popular with the people, and his friends remained true to him until the end.

LOUIS PHILIPPE JOSEPH DE ROFFIGNAC
1820 - 1828

Louis Philippe Joseph de Roffignac was considered a highly successful mayor. So much so, he was remembered long after his death. He was born in France and came to New Orleans as a means of survival. His godmother and godfather, the Duke and Duchess of Orleans, became the king and queen of France. Unfortunately, their fate was the guillotine. Many of those close to the royal family were fearful of the same fate and left the country.

From the very beginning of his residency in New Orleans, Roffignac was, as we say today, well-heeled. His education was extensive and his interests lay in politics. He served 10 years in the legislature, was director of Louisiana State Bank, and a colonel in the Louisiana Legion. These were just a few of his powerful associations and interests. With the necessary funds and right political connections, he had little trouble getting elected mayor. During his term, some streets of New Orleans were paved and lighted for the first time. Until that time, the streets looked like canals after even a slight rain. Because of lack of drainage, they remained a sea of mud for days at a time. Before the lights were installed, everyone who moved around after dark carried a lantern to light the way. Another improvement that proved to be of great importance was the extension of the levees on the riverfront. When all was ready to begin the levee job, it was learned the city did not have sufficient funds to do the work. Roffignac made an appointment to see Nicholas Girod. The current mayor convinced the ex-mayor that, by underwriting the cost of this important project, it would show that he was as good a citizen as he was mayor. Yes, Roffignac, in addition to all of his money, also had a silver tongue.

It was during Roffignac's term in office that the immensely popular General Lafayette visited New Orleans. They were old friends. As a gesture of friendship, the Cabildo-City Hall was converted into a residence for Lafayette. It was renamed for the occasion "Hotel de Ville".

While still serving as mayor, Roffignac decided to pay a visit to his native land. He was determined to go, and, therefore, resigned his office as mayor.

He spent the balance of his life in France, where he lived in splendor. During the time he had left, he followed his interests of literary and social pursuits. The circumstances of his death were rather peculiar. While seated in his invalid chair examining a loaded pistol, he suffered a stroke, falling from the chair. When he hit the ground, the pistol fired. The projectile struck him in the head, causing instant death.

There was one other area where Roffignac was remembered by the citizens. It was in the spirits. Not the religious, but the liquid kind. While still mayor of the city, a new cocktail was invented and named in his honor. The cocktail was made by

pouring a jigger of cognac into a highball glass, adding a portion of raspberry or grenadine syrup, ice, soda and water. It was said that anyone who could drink three of these potent cocktails in quick succession could be mayor for the day.

STITH AND MAESTRI
1858 - 1860
1936 - 1946

COMPLETE OPPOSITES EXCEPT IN RESULTS

If there were ever complete opposites in two men who served as mayor, it would have to be Bob Maestri and Gerard Stith. To begin with, they served in different centuries. In reference to dress, Maestri could be outfitted with the finest suit of clothes made by man and he would still look like a rag doll. Stith could be outfitted in rags and after a few alterations would look like a million dollars. He was affectionately called by those who knew him, "Dapper Dan".

Maestri benefitted from a political war between his idol, Huey Long, and New Orleans Mayor T. Semmes Walmsley. Walmsley couldn't take the heat (politically, that is) and resigned, leaving the doors of City Hall wide open for Bob Maestri to literally walk in. Being unopposed, there was no election, and Maestri became the mayor without uttering a word in his own behalf. He did make one promise to the people. It was in reference to the city's deplorable financial status. The city was bankrupt. Being one of the city's largest property owners, he pledged that if the city was not out of the red by the time he left office, he would use his own vast fortune to pay the city's debts. Stith, on the other hand, was a superb orator and used his verbal skills often and effectively. He also had an extensive educational background while Maestri had very, very little formal education.

Even though the two men were as different as night and day in almost every respect, they were both far above average when rating New Orleans mayors. Each achieved great things during their tenures. Stith was responsible for numerous public improvements during his term. All of this was accomplished during trying times in the city's political history. His greatest achievement was helping reform the police department. Not many men could have accomplished what Stith did in this area of need.

Maestri's major contribution was his ability to raise the city from bankruptcy back to financial respect in just two short years. Under his capable leadership, many improvements were made in many areas of the city that had been neglected for so long. Before he left office, New Orleans was honored by receiving the title "America's Most Improved City".

Capable men like Stith and Maestri seem to come to the forefront when the city is in dire need. Let us hope there is someone on the horizon like this ready to take control and bring the city back to the greatness it once enjoyed.

CITY DIVIDED INTO THREE SECTORS

Even though New Orleanians could unify and help their neighbors in Texas, South America and Central America, the Creoles and Americans were as incompatible as oil and water. They didn't mix well and were constantly at odds with each other.

The Creoles were "a warm-hearted generation" and a "mild and amiable people with much less energy and irascibility than the immigrants from other states", noted observers who came to New Orleans. The only contact the Creoles had with Americans prior to the Louisiana Purchase was the rivermen. They were as crude and unrefined as the Creoles were refined and cultured. After the 1803 Louisiana Purchase, the proud Creoles were to be outnumbered by the continued influx of people arriving from Europe and other sections of the United States. In the 1830s, an incident occurred that was to tear the city asunder. It was a duel between a Creole and an American.

The Creole got the better of his opponent and he thrust his sword through his adversary. He then put his foot on his opponent's chest and then pulled it out. The American fell. He was dead before he hit the ground. The Creole was brought to trial and was acquitted by a Creole judge. A mob of angry Americans, friends of the victim, retaliated by attacking the judge at his home. Tensions between the two factions were at a fevered pitch. The lid was about to blow off the city. To defuse the situation, state authorities withdrew the city charter and provided another. By this move, the city was divided into three separate municipalities. There was one mayor, but each

municipality had its own separate council, recorder, police force and taxing power. This highly unorthodox political hodgepodge lasted an agonizing 16 years. In 1852, a new city charter returned the city government to a single municipality.

MARTIN BEHRMAN
1904 - 1920
1925 - 1926

WESTBANKER

It may be hard to fathom, but there are some New Orleanians who do not know Orleans Parish, that is, the City of New Orleans, is located partially on the westbank as well as on the eastbank of the river. There are some natives that are surprised to learn that the versatile and energetic mayor who served the longest was from the area known as Algiers, located on the westbank. Three separate records were set by this dynamic westbanker. He was not only the only mayor from the westbank, but he also served 17 years in the office. He holds the all-time longevity record in this area. He not only served four terms (16 years) consecutively; he was re-elected after being out of office for five years. Unfortunately, he died before he completed his fifth term. Behrman also has the unenviable distinction of being the only mayor to die while in office.

Martin was, to say the least, the most popular mayor ever elected. He was an astute politician, who, like no other politician before or since, built a political machine called the "Old Regulars". It was in every aspect as powerful and as well known as the political machine built by Mayor Daley in Chicago.

Behrman's contributions to enhancing the city's image were numerous. Some of the advances made during his administration were as follows:

Pure filtered water was available to all homes by a new system of steel piping.

Outdoor cisterns were outlawed. This helped to control the mosquito problem.

A badly needed sewerage system was installed and has been successfully operating ever since. This reduced the death rate considerably.

Tremendous expansion of port facilities.

Institution of the Public Belt Railroad. The port expansion and Public Belt Railroad allowed the city to increase its import-export trade from 283 million to 542 million dollars per year.

Construction of a public library at Lee Circle.

New annex added to City Hall.

Construction of new courthouse building on Royal Street.

A massive palatial marble post office and federal court building constructed.

Twenty-four new schools built, including four much-needed high schools.

Improved fire and police departments.

Creation of the Parkway Commission.

The above is just a smithering of what was accomplished by this political dynamo. He died on January 12, 1926. Like other great political, civic and military leaders before him, namely,

Louisiana Governor Isaac Johnson, Jefferson Davis, President of the Confederacy, General P. G. T. Beauregard, and David C. Hennessey, New Orleans' first Chief of Police, Behrman was honored by lying in state in the council chamber of Gallier (old city hall) Hall. While there, his body was reviewed by 20,000 grief-stricken citizens.

Behrman was only 61 years old when he breathed his last breath. As one man put it, "Cause of his death - overwork. He died a martyr to his city. One can only surmise what additional great things he would have accomplished had he served out his fifth or possibly even sixth terms".

A writer who best summed up Martin Behrman was quoted, "in all facets Behrman was a pioneer in the modern administration of the office of mayor, and during his tenure he envisioned or made plans for many of the improvements which followed many years later. Above all, honesty, good government, sound management were his main assets. The desire to help both the 'little' man and the 'big' man further endeared him".

VIC SCHIRO
1961 - 1970

Just as Martin Behrman was considered the most-popular mayor, Vic Schiro would have to be classified the most beloved. During his terms in office, chances are there was not a ribbon he did not cut, a carnival ball he did not attend, a parade he did not ride in or a new baby he did not kiss. Someone jokingly said Vic

was like a New Orleans roach, he was everywhere. Yes, he was also every bit as resilient. Of all his media presence, his most visible, and it appears most enjoyable time was when the city prepared for or suffered a hurricane. He would put on his hard hat and spend more time on TV than any news reporter. He was seen on the TV screen at City Hall working diligently outlining the necessary preparations. Next, he was seen at the hurricane command center at the end of West End-Pontchartrain Boulevards supervising the activities. He was filmed in his limousine going from one place to another. The next time you saw him he was in an army duck (half boat half truck) cruising flooded areas helping people evacuate. Toward the end of the disaster he would be shown flying over the area evaluating the damages and securing necessary data to apply for federal disaster relief funds for his people. It appeared Vic thrived during these trying times.

One statement Vic made on TV during a hurricane threat became his all-time classic. He told the TV audience "There are a lot of rumors floating around out there. Don't believe any of them unless you hear them from me." The TV stations, of course, ran it over and over and over and over.

Another of the colorful stories told of Vic happened in 1968, the year New Orleans celebrated its 250th birthday. Since the exact date of the city's founding was not known (the ship carrying the records back to France sank in a hurricane), the joke going around was that Vic used his diplomacy in selecting the date by putting tickets for each day of the month in one hat and for each month of the year in another. He then reached in and pulled out the date and the month for the celebration to take place. Accordingly, New Orleans' birthday from that date forward has been celebrated on August 6-7/8, the mayor's hat size.

The Louisiana Historical Society believes the date was either February 9, 10, or 11 of 1718.

No one can deny Vic's dedication to the City of New Orleans. He will always be loved and affectionately remembered for his dedication to and his love of this city.

THREE MAYORS IN ONE DAY!!!
1936

In 1936, a most unusual incident, unequalled in American politics, took place at City Hall in New Orleans.

Mayor T. Semmes Walmsley's (called "Turkey Head" by his bitter political enemy Huey Long) roller coaster ride as mayor was about to come to an abrupt end. On June 30 of that year, he handed in his official resignation. This was not his first

A. MILES PRATT   JESSE S. CAVE   FRED A. EARHART

but second attempt to resign his position. The first was two years earlier. Provisoes attached to that offer to resign were not met, and his resignation did not go into effect.

On June 30, 1936, Walmsley's resignation was accepted, placing Finance Commissioner A. Miles Pratt in the position of Acting Mayor. Two weeks later, on July 15, 1936, Pratt was offered the position as Collector of Customs for the Port of New Orleans. There was no way he was going to pass up that lucrative plum. He resigned and was succeeded as Acting Mayor by Jesse S. Cave, who, for unknown reasons a few hours after being sworn in as Acting Mayor, resigned the position, with Fred A. Earhart taking over the duties of Acting Mayor.

On July 15, 1936, New Orleans had the unique distinction of having been served by three different mayors in one day.

AUGUSTINE MC CARTY
1815 - 1820

POSSIBLE RELIEF
TURNS INTO QUICK DISBELIEF!

Because of the city's hot and humid climate, New Orleanians undoubtedly became ecstatic when they found out in the early 1800s that relief was finally on its way. A sailing ship was headed for New Orleans loaded to the gunwales with ice taken from the frozen lakes of Maine.

Upon its arrival, a large crowd gathered at the levee. Their great excitement was, unfortunately, short-lived. As soon as the ship was moored, New Orleans Mayor Augustine McCarty, with a police escort, went on board. The mayor quickly told the cheering citizens, "As your duly elected mayor, my duty compels me to protect you even though what I am about to do will be unpopular." He then ordered the police to throw the ice overboard. The crowd quickly went from cheers to jeers. In unison, the irate mob demanded to know why he had done such a dastardly deed. The mayor quickly responded, "The city's medical supervisor has advised me that medical scientists believe a cold substance taken into the human body will induce tuberculosis." The crowd's response no doubt was "bah-humbug". The first shipload of ice that brought possible relief turned the city into disbelief.

JOHN FITZPATRICK
1892 - 1896

N. O. GARBAGE BARGES
MAKE NEWS IN 19TH CENTURY

Up until 1893, when New Orleans first disposed of garbage through incineration, all garbage disposal was handled in the following manner.

A small army of sanitation department personnel with garbage carts went from door to door collecting refuse. From there, it was brought to three different locations along the river and put on the city's garbage barges. It was then taken down river, below Chalmette, where it was dumped into the river in hopes the current would, in a sense, flush it into the Gulf of Mexico.

One serious problem with the system was encountered. In the eyes of the city fathers, the fun-loving, let-the-good-times-roll New Orleanians were misusing these vehicles of garbage conveyance. To eliminate this unusual problem, a law was hastily passed and strongly enforced. The law stated, "No picnics or dances will be allowed on the city's garbage barges under penalty of heavy fines."

It looks like history is repeating itself. Today our city fathers have put Lakeshore Drive off-limits during evening hours to the fun-loving, let-the-good-times-roll Orleanians, just as the garbage barges were put off-limits in years gone by.

What's a body to do to have fun these days?

HOW THEY ARE REMEMBERED

Through the years, mayors of the city have been honored in numerous ways. The number one type of remembrance is in street names. Examples: Girod, Prieur, Genois, Freret, Montegut, Behrman, McShane, O'Keefe, Walmsley, Pratt and Earhart. In more recent times, Dutch Morial's name has been affixed to the new convention center, and the walk adjacent to the French Quarter across from Jackson Square was named the

Moon Walk in honor of Mayor Landrieu. Bob Maestri had a bridge named in his honor, Behrman a gymnasium. Pitot House on Bayou St. John is visited by thousands of visitors each year. Schools were named de Boré, Crossman, Wiltz, Capdeville and Behrman. Behrman also has a park, and so do Girod and Shakspeare.

MAYOR CHEP MORRISON
1946 - 1961

COOL MAYOR WHO GOT IN HOT WATER

From the time of the first Rex Parade in 1872, the four major Mardi Gras Krewes, Rex, Comus, Proteus and Momus, have used what has been considered the traditional Carnival and Mardi Gras parade route. The route is as follows:

Up St. Charles Avenue to near Louisiana Avenue, then back down St. Charles Avenue and around Lee Circle, past Gallier Hall (the old City Hall) to Canal Street and on to their ball locations.

It was also customary from the very first Rex parade that the king of Mardi Gras propose a toast to city officials at City Hall.

When Mayor de Lesseps "Chep" Morrison completed his new and futuristic civic center, he was as proud as a peacock. The tall, modern city hall was its brightest jewel. Chep no doubt thought that by re-routing the Carnival and Mardi Gras parades right through the civic center (fully a mile out of the way), the traditional toast could be made in front of the new City Hall and this would allow him to show off his latest accomplishment. The captains of the various krewes were not especially keen on this idea. In fact, they were downright opposed to it. Chep was a strong-willed person and reminded the captains that in order to obtain a parade permit the city's full cooperation was required. Chep held the trump card. The captains of the various krewes had no other choice. They did, although reluctantly, change their routes and passed in front of the new City Hall. In a sense, the mayor simply blackmailed the captains into carrying out his wishes. When parade time rolled around, the masses of people who attended the parades were

not as receptive or intimidated into accepting the new route. Like stubborn mules, they would not accept this departure from tradition. Although the krewes changed their parade route to please the mayor, the people did not show up at the new Civic Center. The old die-hard traditionalists simply went to Gallier Hall, the old City Hall, where they had gone for so many years.

As the old saying goes, if you don't succeed the first time, try and try again. The next year, the city again tried to entice the multitudes to come to the new civic center. The results of the second attempt were less successful than the first. Because of the wishes of the people, through non-participation, the city allowed the captains to go back to the old traditional parade route. One old timer said, "Chep would have had an easier time passing a new tax, and you know how New Orleanians hate taxes, than he had trying to change one of our sacred Mardi Gras traditions."

You could say the people of New Orleans sang "Don't Mess with My Parade Route" long before the current popular song "Don't Mess with My Tu Tu" was ever written.

JOSEPH A. SHAKSPEARE
1880 - 1882
1888 - 1892

Since the very first Rex parade in 1872, only one New Orleans mayor, Joseph A. Shakspeare, (1882) served as king of Mardi Gras.

MAYOR
AND KING

CITY HALL
ONLY THREE STRUCTURES SERVED AS CITY HALL

CABILDO
1803-1853

GALLIER HALL
1853-1957

PRESENT CITY HALL
1957 —

Over the past 190 years, only three buildings have served as City Hall. In spite of all of the political wars, all three structures are still standing and in daily use.

1803 - 1853   CABILDO
1853 - 1957   GALLIER HALL
1957 - PRESENT   CITY HALL

ORLEANS PARISH

Louisiana is the only state of the 50 that is divided politically into parishes.

Orleans Parish is the smallest of the 64 in area and is the largest in population. It is also the only parish that encompasses an entire city.

The 64 original skyboxes in the Louisiana Superdome are named for the 64 parishes in Louisiana. There is no doubt that the Louisiana Superdome is surrounded by politics. It is obvious in the political street names that surround it. (See drawing on next page).

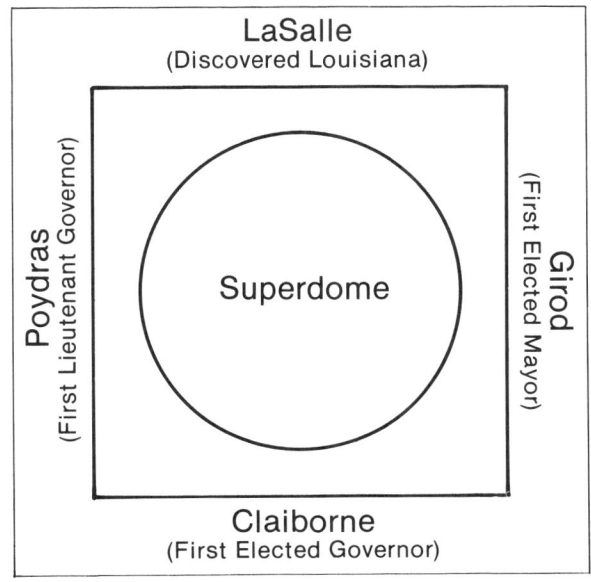

NEW ORLEANS FIRST CENSUS
& POPULATION FIGURES

The city's political leaders were "Johnny-on-the-Spot" reference keeping track of those entrusted to their care. This, no doubt, was to guarantee that everyone who was required to pay taxes did so.

Reference taxes: If our forefathers thought taxation without representation was bad, they should be around today.

The first complete census for New Orleans was signed by Inspector General of Troops in Louisiana, Sieur Deron d'Artauguette, on November 24, 1721. The figures were as follows:

293 men
140 women
 96 children
155 French servants   514 negro slaves
684 Total   51 indian slaves
                                 565 Total

NEW ORLEANS POPULATION THROUGH THE YEARS

1810- 17,242	1880-216,090	1950-570,445
1820- 27,176	1890-242,039	1960-627,525
1830- 46,082	1900-287,104	1970-593,471
1840-102,193	1910-339,075	1980-557,927
1850-116,375	1920-387,219	1990-496,938
1860-168,675	1930-458,762	
1870-191,418	1940-494,537	

ONE OF THE CITY'S BEST BUYS

On June 18, 1852, John Douglas was authorized to design an official seal for the City of New Orleans. Mr. Douglas

wasted no time. In just eight days, his design was completed and approved. The official seal contains the following:

- 31 stars for the 31 states then in the Union. ·
- 12 stars in an inner circle at the top and one at its center which represent the original 13 states.

- 12 stars in an outer circle are for 12 states admitted into the Union from March 4, 1791, to June 15, 1836.
- 3 stars at bottom left and bottom right represent six states admitted from January 26, 1837, to September 9, 1850.
- The center shows two Indians beside three wigwams, over which the sun's rays are slanting.
- An alligator at bottom center brings to mind the swamps of Louisiana.
- Reclining prominently at center is a white-bearded Neptune, mythical god of waters and the sea, representing Old Man River.

According to city records, Mr. Douglas received a whopping $16 for the design, engraving dye and printing of the seal. Chances are, this was one of the best buys (cost 12 cents' per year) the city has ever made.

MAYORS OF NEW ORLEANS
1803-PRESENT

Names	From	To
Etienne de Boré	11/30/1803	5/26/1804
James Pitot	6/2/1804	7/26/1805
John Watkins	7/27/1805	3/8/1807
James J. Mather	3/9/1807	5/16/1812
Charles Trudeau (Acting Mayor)	5/16/1812	10/8/1812
Nicholas Girod	10/8/1812	9/4/1815
Le Breton Dorgenois	11/6/1812	12/4/1812
(Acting Mayor)		
Augustine McCarty	9/4/1815	5/13/1820
Joseph Roffignac	5/14/1820	5/10/1828
Denis Prieur	5/12/1828	4/9/1838
Paul Bertus (Acting Mayor)	4/10/1838	5/12/1838
Charles Genois	5/12/1838	4/6/1840
(No records available)	4/7/1840	5/10/1840
William Freret	5/11/1840	4/4/1842
Denis Prieur	4/4/1842	2/7/1843
Paul Bertus (Acting Mayor)	2/7/1843	2/26/1843
William Freret	2/27/1843	5/12/1844

Joseph Edgard Montegut	5/13/1844	4/5/1846
Abdil Daily Crossman	5/11/1846	3/26/1854
John L. Lewis	4/10/1854	6/17/1856
Charles M. Waterman	6/17/1856	6/8/1858
Gerard Stith	6/21/1858	6/18/1860
John T. Monroe	6/18/1860	5/16/1862
MILITARY MAYORS	**5/20/1862**	**3/27/1866**
George F. Shepley (Acting Mayor)	5/20/1862	7/11/1862
Godfrey Weitzel (Acting Mayor)	7/14/1862	8/5/1862
Jonas H. French (Acting Mayor)	8/6/1862	8/20/1862
Godfrey Weitzel (Acting Mayor)	8/21/1862	9/30/1862
Henry C. Deming (Acting Mayor)	10/2/1862	1/30/1863
James F. Miller (Acting Mayor)	1/30/1862	9/12/1863
E. H. Durell (Acting Mayor)	9/12/1863	10/30/1863
James F. Miller (Acting Mayor)	11/6/1863	2/2/1864
Stephen Hoyt (Acting Mayor)	2/9/1864	3/21/1865
Hugh Kennedy (Acting Mayor)	3/21/1865	5/5/1865
Samuel Miller Quincy (Acting Mayor)	5/5/1865	6/8/1865
Glendy Burke (Acting Mayor)	6/8/1865	6/28/1865
Hugh Kennedy (Acting Mayor)	6/28/1865	3/18/1866
J. Ad. Rozier (Acting Mayor)	3/19/1866	3/20/1866
George Clark (Acting Mayor)	3/20/1866	5/11/1866
John T. Monroe	5/12/1866	3/28/1867
Edward Heath	3/28/1867	6/10/1868
John R. Conway	6/10/1868	4/4/1870
Benjamin Franklin Flanders	4/4/1870	11/29/1872
Louis A. Wiltz	11/30/1872	11/30/1874
Charles J. Leeds	11/30/1874	12/19/1876
Edward Pilsbury	12/19/1876	11/18/1878
Isaac W. Patton	11/18/1878	12/16/1880
Joseph A. Shakspeare	12/16/1880	11/20/1882
W. J. Behan	11/20/1882	4/28/1884
J. Valsin Guillotte	4/29/1884	4/23/1888
Joseph A. Shakspeare	4/24/1888	4/25/1892
John Fitzpatrick	4/25/1892	4/27/1896
Walter C. Flower	4/27/1896	5/7/1900

Paul Capdeville	5/7/1900	12/5/1904
Martin Behrman	12/5/1904	12/6/1920
Andrew J. McShane	12/6/1920	5/4/1925
Martin Behrman	5/4/1925	1/12/1926
Arthur J. O'Keefe (Acting Mayor)	1/12/1926	3/15/1926
Arthur J. O'Keefe (Resigned)	3/15/1926	2/14/1930
T. Semmes Walmsley (Acting Mayor)	7/15/1929	5/5/1930
T. Semmes Walmsley	5/5/1930	6/30/1936
A. Miles Pratt (Acting Mayor)	6/30/1936	7/15/1936
Fred A. Earhart (Acting Mayor)	7/15/1936	7/15/1936
Jesse S. Cave (Acting Mayor)	7/15/1936	8/17/1936
Robert S. Maestri	8/18/1936	5/6/1946
de Lesseps Morrison	5/6/1946	6/14/1961
Victor Hugo Schiro	6/21/1961	5/1/1970
Landrieu	5/4/1970	5/2/1978
Ernest "Dutch" Morial	5/2/1978	5/5/1986
Sidney Barthelemy	5/5/1986	5/5/94
Marc Morial	5/5/1994	present

POLITICS
NEW ORLEANS' NUMBER ONE SPORT

It has been said, and rightfully so, that the number one sport in New Orleans is not football, baseball, boxing or basketball. As popular as hunting and fishing have been through the years, they too are not the number one sport. The city's number one sport is now and always has been politics. Politics, like the rest of the city's makeup, is far different from politics of other cities throughout the country. The reason for the difference is that, from almost the beginning, the city's residents were from all continents of the world. This phenomenon still exists with the most recent influx of a large number of Vietnamese. Not only did each contingent bring its own speech pattern and favorite food selection, they also brought their individual country's political ideology. Upon arrival, they were anxious and willing to offer all that they had, including their politics, to their newly adopted homeland. I think all will agree, the city's food is unique, natives do not speak with a southern drawl as found in other southern cities, and, for sure, politics is not only different but is practiced with a passion unequaled even in any XXX rated movie. All of these differences is what makes New Orleans the unique city that it is. It would not be fair or wise to knock the differences, for over the years people from all six continents visit, enjoy, and upon leaving, anxiously await their next visit.

Yes, as Orleanians proudly proclaim "vive la difference", even when it comes to politics.

CITY HALL HUMOR

Just as we started this chapter with a tongue-in-cheek story, let us end it the same way.

In the men's room at City Hall, in order to reduce overhead on paper towels, the city purchased electric hand dryers. Someone, no doubt knowing the personnel in the office, put up a sign over the hand dryer that stated, "For a Message from your Mayor or City Council Members Please Push Button."

CHAPTER TWO

TRANSPORTATION

INTRODUCTION

Prior to the Louisiana Purchase in 1803, the French Quarter, for all practical purposes, was the City of New Orleans. As such, it covered a relatively small area. Its boundaries were, and still are, from the Mississippi River to Rampart Street, and from Esplanade Avenue to Canal Street. The short distances that people were required to travel to get around town did not present a transportation problem to the majority of its early dwellers.

It was not until after the Louisiana Purchase when the first steamboat arrived in 1812, coupled with increased traffic brought on by the Pontchartrain Railroad Station located close to the French Quarter in 1832, that transportation problems became apparent. Those three events led to large numbers of people from outside the city boundaries entering the Quarter to transact business. Outsiders also came to the Quarter to dine and seek other forms of entertainment.

The more affluent Quarter residents all had riding horses and horse-drawn carriages for their convenience. The normal

layout for a family with financial means was to build a multistory building with a carriage way and a storage area for the carriage as part of the overall plan. Many such structures allowed the men to conduct their business on the ground level, with living quarters on the upper levels. The carriage way led to a patio with a two-story building in the rear of the property. On the first level, the carriage and horses were housed. The kitchen was also located on the ground floor next to the carriage storage area (stable). All food was cooked in the kitchen and carried to the dining area of the main house. The purpose of separating the structures was twofold—first, to keep the main house from getting hot in the summer months, and secondly, as a safety precaution. Without a paid fire department, great pains were taken to protect the main houses from fire. The slave quarters were always located above the stable and kitchen.

OMNIBUSES
FIRST PUBLIC RAPID TRANSIT

Because of the large influx of nonresidents in the French Quarter after the Louisiana Purchase, New Orleans' first transportation system was started. The fare in 1832 was 12½ cents. The service began with two small horse-drawn vehicles. The line ran from Canal to Chartres, down Chartres to Place d' Armes (Jackson Square), then to the cotton presses on Levee

Street. From there it went to the Pontchartrain Railroad depot. Due to the vehicles' limited carrying capacity, in a very short time the service was overloaded. The owners of the line resolved the problem almost immediately. The Louisiana Advertiser newspaper ran an article stating that the two small omnibuses were to be replaced. The new vehicles, built by Messrs. Carters of New York, arrived in New Orleans and were hastily put into service. They were named "Cotton Plant" and "Tobacco Plant". Each carried 14 passengers, with enough room for them to be comfortably seated. The vehicles were each pulled by four horses.

It wasn't long before other entrepreneurs realized this new service was a great way to generate profits. Within a short time, 12 new lines were covering the entire city. Service in the French Quarter began at 7:00 a.m. and stopped at 7:30 p.m. As an additional service to their customers, the omnibuses also carried letter boxes. For the comfort of its female passengers, a sign in the carriage requested that gentlemen not smoke in deference to ladies.

Steel rail lines

STEEL RAIL LINES

The population in New Orleans at the end of the 1830s was 46,082. In the 1840s, it jumped to 102,193. By the 1850s, with the population still growing, it was decided that the old-fashioned omnibuses no longer satisfied the rising demand. Research proved that iron wheels on iron rails enabled a horse to pull a heavy load faster and with less effort. With this new-found knowledge, construction began. Before long, steel rails covered the city like a giant spider web.

WALKING CAR?

Prior to electrification, inventors were constantly looking for more dependable means of propulsion than the ornery mules that often lived up to their reputation of being cantankerous and unbelievably stubborn. In 1866, a rather strange and unsuccessful attempt at replacing the mules was introduced. The "walking car", as it was called, was operated by a

motorman turning a crank at the front of the car. The crank was connected to two long scissor-like arms that turned a rimless wheel at the rear of the car. The wheel had heavy spokes, with each spoke having an iron ball on the end. As the wheel turned, the ball would catch in the ground and push the car forward. As the inventor proudly put it, "The walking car had the same or better speed as that of a mule pulling the car.'' Although it did work as the inventor said it would, the motorman, in performing the unpleasant, tiring, monotonous duty, became more cantankerous than the stubborn mules. They protested, stating, "No one would make jackasses out of us."

WATER TRANSPORTATION

With so many miles of canals, it should come as no surprise that New Orleans at one time did have a barge transportation line. In the 1840s, this unusual mode of transportation began carrying passengers and carriages on the New Basin Canal (present route of the Pontchartrain Expressway and part of the interstate system). Barges were towed from Rampart Street to the lakefront by mules walking along the bank. Fare for this means of transportation was only 20 cents. It was cheaper than the Pontchartrain Railroad that ran from the river to the lake, down present-day Elysian Fields Avenue. The service ran until just before the Civil War. After the war ended, service was resumed but did not survive for very long.

This mode of transportation, although discontinued in New Orleans, is still in existence (with mechanical propulsion) in both Amsterdam and Venice.

THE NEW ORLEANS CAR TRACTION COMPANY

General P. G. T. Beauregard's firing of the first shot on Fort Sumter started the Civil War. The Civil War, unfortunately, lasted longer than Beauregard's company, the New Orleans Car Traction Company. It was chartered March 29, 1870. It was considered by some to be bizarre. Others thought his idea was fantastic. Most agreed it was "way-out". The idea is best described by comparing it to the present-day San Francisco cable cars. Beauregard's idea was to support a cable above the railroad tracks instead of in the ground as was done in San Francisco. Two stationary steam locomotives were used to keep the cable in constant motion. When the conductor wanted the car to move, he would pull a lever that would clamp onto the cable. When he wanted to stop for traffic or to pick up passengers, he would release the lever. For six months, the line was put into daily operation. Even though the equipment worked as it was supposed to, economically it was not a success.

"Fireless Engine" Using Condensed Steam. Boiler Was Filled at Terminals. One of the Many Unsuccessful Transportation Experiments Preceding the Trolley.

Just think, had Beauregard made one single change, that of putting the cable below the track instead of overhead, he might have reduced the cost of operation, and the line would possibly still be in business today.

PNEUMATIC-AMMONIA-ELECTRIC-BATTERY!!!

In December of 1872, yet another reason to find other means of propulsion to replace the cantankerous mules occurred. The city was stricken with an "epizooty" epidemic. This epidemic, unlike the numerous yellow fever epidemics that infected humans, epizooty attacked the entire city's population of beasts of burden. All transit lines came to a complete stop. For one week, nothing moved that was pulled by animals.

One company came up with the idea of pneumatic propulsion. It was as successful as the Ammonia Motor and Railway Company. The most impressive thing about that company was the names of the men who organized it. Their names and the names in the social register were for the most part one and the same. Unfortunately, they put their capital to work, but the Ammonia Motor and Railway Company's new invention didn't.

Another new method of propulsion tried was the use of electric batteries. It may have been a shocking idea, but it didn't work either.

FIRST ELECTRIC STREETCARS IN NORTH AMERICA

In 1884, New Orleans hosted a World's Fair. The location was the site of present-day Audubon Park. Previous to the fair,

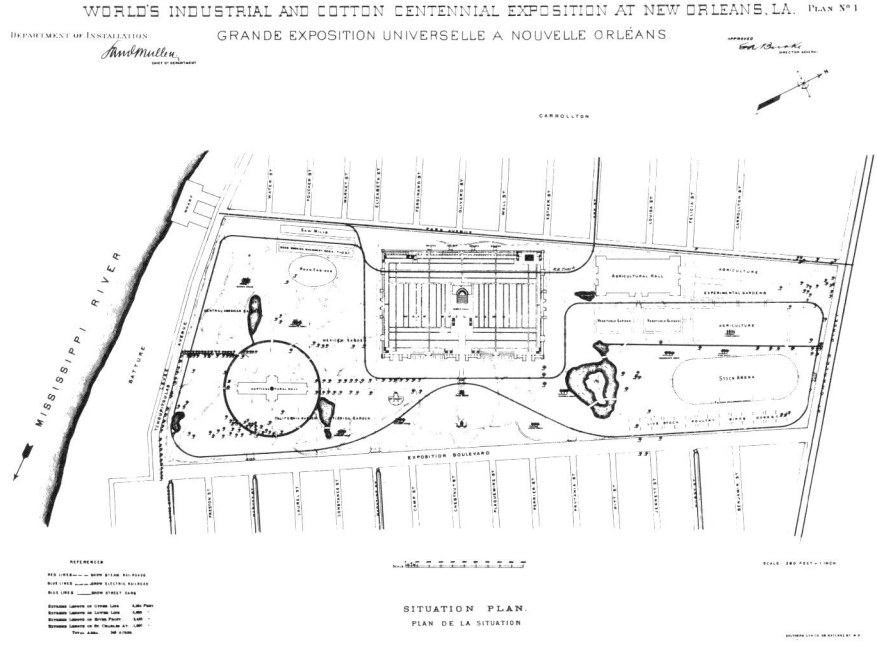

the grounds were that of upper City Park. Prior to that, it was the plantation of New Orleans' first appointed mayor, Etienne de Boré. Just as de Boré had the dubious distinction of being the first man in history to granulate sugar commercially, the

1884 World's Fair also enjoyed numerous firsts. A few examples: it had the largest building ever built for a world's fair. The main building covered 33 acres under one roof. This massive building was also the first world's fair building to be lighted by electric lights. It was illuminated by 5,000 light bulbs. This in itself was impressive. New Orleans, at the time, landwise, was the largest city in the United States and had only 500 street lights to illuminate the entire city. The main building was also mechanically cooled by overhead ceiling fans. They were operated by many miles of shafting that crisscrossed the building like a giant grid. In each of the four corners of the building, electric elevators carried visitors to the upper galleries. From there they could see all exhibits with a bird's eye view.

Another first, and the most visible, was the dual electric railway system that ran throughout the grounds. The first was operated by the Daft Electric Light Company. The system was patented by Mr. Leo Daft. The principle for this system was a third rail located in the center of the track. It carried the electric current needed to operate the streetcar. The Daft Company generated the necessary electricity by use of a huge dynamo.

There was sufficient electricity generated to operate not only the streetcars, but lights installed along the line as well. The second system was installed by a Belgian company headed by Mr. Charles J. Van de Poeles. The system utilized the overhead trolley method of transmitting power. It did not take long to prove to be the more efficient and maintenance free to operate. It also generated far more riders than its competition. The Belgians' operation was spectacular with its motor car and two large open cars traveling three miles at a nominal cost. Each trip lasted 30 minutes. The schedule of runs was frequent, leaving every two to three minutes. As the cars traveled around the grounds, they made stops at all points of major interest.

One visitor who later became world-renowned became infatuated with this new mode of transportation. He stayed much longer than his original itinerary called for. During his stay in New Orleans, he operated the overhead trolley car on numerous occasions. His name, Sir Thomas Lipton of Lipton Tea fame. It is interesting to note that when New Orleans hosted the 1984 World's Fair, Lipton Tea had a large display area.

The overhead electric trolley system proved to be so successful many other major cities throughout the country put it into service as early as 1886. New Orleans, although the first to have a successful electric trolley system, waited until 1893 before it jumped on the electric trolley bandwagon. It was just another incident in the city's history that confirms that it is a city of procrastination. On the other hand, in the long run it may not be a negative but a positive way of doing things. Remember, the St. Charles streetcar is the longest continuously running streetcar line anywhere in the world.

February 1, 1893, St. Charles Line first in New Orleans to be electrified.

NEW ORLEANS' OLDEST
ELECTRIC STREETCAR LINE

July 13, 1890, silver spike ceremony.

Construction of the city's first permanent electric streetcar line started with a silver spike ceremony held at Lee Circle on July 13, 1890. The system was completed in 1893. The Carrollton Line (renamed "St. Charles" on day of electrification) officially began service on February 1, 1893, with a parade of seven cars. The Picayune on February 1, 1893, comments thusly:

"Electric cars are started on St. Charles Avenue. They create as much excitement as a Rex parade. Yesterday for the first time, New Orleans rode by wire. The experience proved delightful, safe, and successful."

STREETCAR NAMED DESIRE

The streetcar named Desire became famous worldwide thanks to Tennessee Williams' hit play "A Streetcar Named Desire". The line began operation on October 17, 1920. It dropped its passengers off at the bars and night clubs along Bourbon Street and the shopping district along Royal Street. It also traveled to the densely populated area along the lower portion of its route. The very last run for the Desire streetcar was May 30, 1948. Although it has not run its regular route for 45 years, it is still a sightseer's delight. Presently, it is on display in the rear of the U.S. Mint on Esplanade Avenue. Its present permanent location is just a few blocks from where it ran for so many years. Tennessee Williams, who immortalized the streetcar in writing his hit play and using the name of the line, was a

resident of the French Quarter. He not only lived in the Quarter, but he was quoted as saying he "loved, admired and was inspired by its charm."

AROUND THE BELT
THE ST. CHARLES AND TULANE

Both of these lines were started on February 19, 1900, and lasted almost 51 years. The last run of both lines was on January 8, 1951. It was on that date the Tulane streetcar trolley line was replaced with trackless trolleys (buses). The St. Charles belt covered 12½ miles beginning on Canal Street, up Baronne to Howard Avenue, St. Charles Avenue, Carrollton Avenue, Tulane Avenue, S. Rampart Street, back to Canal Street.

The Tulane belt covered 11.229 miles. Its route was as follows. From a loop at foot of Canal, out Canal, S. Rampart, Tulane, Carrollton Avenue, St. Charles Avenue, Howard Avenue, Baronne back to Canal. The streetcar route on Baronne Street from Howard Avenue to Canal was changed to Carondelet Street sometime after service began.

The story of the St. Charles belt line was written in numerous publications years ago as being one of the best buys available when visiting New Orleans. A short sampling of what was to be seen: You could board the streetcar on Canal Street in downtown New Orleans and get a leisurely, fabulous tour of the city for only seven cents. Just one half block from Canal Street, the first point of interest you passed on Baronne Street was the Church of the Immaculate Conception. This beautiful, Moorish style (or sometimes described as Saracenic or Arabian) church was built by the Society of Jesus, better known as the Jesuits. The Russian dome, high over the altar, was put into the design of the church as a sign of the Jesuit's appreciation for Catherine The Great's efforts on behalf of the order. This was the same order of priests who purchased the first land sold in Louisiana. Their property was what is now called downtown New Orleans. As the streetcar made its swing around Lee Circle, the first sight you would see would be the beautiful city library. It was a gift of philanthropist Andrew Carnegie. The massive structure, costing $375,000 at the turn of the century, was a replica of a famous structure, the Mars Ultor Temple at Rome. As the car began its ride up St. Charles Avenue, the sight of this beautiful residential area was and is still breathtaking. The street is lined with 100-year-old oak trees majestically laden with silvery moss. The street is lined with equally old and majestic Victorian and other architectural treasures. The area is appropriately called the Garden District. Unlike the French Quarter, where the gardens are enclosed behind walls for the benefit of the owners only, the gardens on the avenue are all in front of the houses for everyone's enjoyment. St. Charles Avenue is the location of numerous schools. Loyola and Tulane Universities, as well as St. Mary's Dominican College, are just a few. It must be a very pious as well as academic street, for there are a total of 13 churches and synagogues between Lee Circle and Carrollton Avenue. As you sway from side to side in the shade of the oak trees, you look out the window in awe as you pass the stately old "Orleans Club", an exclusive club for women. A short distance later you see a reproduction of "Tara", the home of Scarlet O'Hara in "Gone With the Wind".

The street is truly a history lesson in itself, for all the streets that cross it have historical names. Many of the families who have lived on the avenue can be found in the city's social register. When first laid out, St. Charles Avenue was named Nyades. The name was chosen because of its close proximity to the river. Nyades, in Greek mythology, was the water god. Even though the name of the street changed and families who have resided there have come and gone, something has remained constant. The avenue has always been a beautiful, peaceful, historical place. It is as popular today with both residents of the city and visitors as it always has been. Might I suggest, at your leisure, you continue the tour? Although the complete belt route no longer exists, you can go as far as Carrollton and Claiborne, where the line ends today. As they say, half a loaf is better than none.

THE LAST RUN WASN'T FUN

The last day of operation of the Canal streetcar line took place on May 31, 1964. The very last run left from the end of the

line at the cemeteries on City Park Avenue, at exactly 3:37 a.m., and headed towards the river. There were 100 passengers, all riding courtesy of an anonymous donor who liked streetcars. As the car swayed back and forth the passengers on board sang "Auld Lang Syne", accompanied by guitars and mandolins. At 4:18 a.m., the car reached Canal and St. Charles Streets. A female passenger got out and placed a wreath of flowers on the neutral ground. With great confidence, she predicted streetcars would someday return.

Twenty-four years later, her prediction came true when the Red Line, which runs parallel to the river alongside the French Quarter, began operation. From the very beginning, it was highly successful, so much so that a short time later additional cars and tracks were put into service to help keep up with the continually growing demand.

There is a strong push being made at this time to put streetcars back in operation. The Canal line is targeted to be the next to be brought back to life. The people who rode the streetcars for years are ecstatic. As one passenger said, "It's true, good things do come to those who wait."

TRANSIT STRIKE
MISFORTUNE LEADS TO GOOD FORTUNE

MISFORTUNE

One of the lengthiest and most-violent transit railway strikes the nation ever experienced began in New Orleans at 10:00 p.m., July 1, 1929. The strike and ensuing violence that took place had nothing to do with money or hours worked. The burr under the union's saddle was over the company's unwillingness to accept the closed-shop provision. The second goal was to curb the company's policy of discharging employees without cause. The strike officially began on July 1st. On July 5, without any agreement being made between the company and the union, an attempt was made by the transit company to reactivate service. This action was met with unbelievable violence. The company's transit vehicles were overturned and set on fire

by crowds of strikers, sympathizers, and out of town "professional" trouble makers. Police, including federal marshals, were called in. Heavily outnumbered, they were unable to protect the street railway service. Tensions were at an all-time high. New Orleans Public Service, Incorporated Vice-President A. B. Patterson and A. F. L. President Green began arbitration. Although an agreement was reached in August, the union members did not agree to go back to work until after they voted on October 10th. At that time, they accepted the Patterson-Green agreement.

NOPSI took a financial beating during the 1929 strike. Forty million fewer riders used the transit system than the previous year.

GOOD FORTUNE

What good fortune, you might ask, could possibly come out of the misfortune just described. It was the beginning of the New Orleans sandwich called the po-boy. Benny and Clovis Martin, owners of Martin Brothers Restaurant on St. Claude Street (Avenue), were grateful for the business they enjoyed. Many of those who frequented their place of business were the street railway workers. With the strike came difficult economic times for these laboring men. Things were already tough because of conditions leading to the depression. The added burden of no take-home pay added to their misery. The two brothers set out to help in any way they could. They decided the best way was to offer an inexpensive sandwich that would prac-

tically feed an entire family. They contacted an Italian baker named Gendusa, and told him of their idea. New Orleans french bread traditionally was short and wide. Gendusa decided he would bake a new loaf that would be much longer (36″-42″) and smaller in diameter. Martin Brothers, as agreed, purchased and cut the bread into 12″-15″ lengths, filled it with gravy, roast beef, mayo, lettuce, tomato and pickles. This they would then sell for a nickel to the poor boys to help them feed their families. The name that stuck from this new New Orleans sandwich creation was the "po boy".

Because of the misfortune of the '29 transit strike, the city's number one sandwich, until this day, was born. Even though the original po boy was made with roast beef, today you must specify the type of po boy you want. You can order the traditional, or ham and swiss, oyster, shrimp, meatball, etc., etc.

Just as the po boy is an ingenious creation of New Orleans, the term dressed, meaning with lettuce and tomato, is also a New Orleans creation. When outside of Louisiana, if you ask for your sandwich dressed, good chances are they think it must be served while wearing a coat and tie.

Martin Brothers' kindness in thinking of their customers was not forgotten. The restaurant became the most popular eating spot in town for many years. Its creation received the greatest compliment available. It was copied by every location in New Orleans and Louisiana, wherever sandwiches were sold. Yes, to be copied is the greatest form of flattery, and yes, misfortune can bring good fortune, as pointed out in this transit strike/sandwich story.

LITTLE KNOWN FACTS

U.S. Mail
From 1902-1924, electric streetcars carried closed pouches of mail from the main post office to various postal branches. When the mail was on board, a red and white sign that read "U.S. Mail" was displayed. The pouches were handled only by post office employees.

War Economy
During the military occupation after New Orleans fell in the Civil War, New Orleans suffered economically. The city's transit lines continued to operate, but had to make concessions in order to stay in business. The decision was made to reduce fares drastically.

1873 Was a Bad Year

Operators of the New Orleans Railroad Company were far from pleased in 1873. The annual report bemoaned "the deplorable financial conditions of the whole community." It further stated that there were 1,128,135 less passengers in 1873 than in 1872. If that wasn't bad enough, they also reported in that same year they collected $2,500.00 in counterfeit nickels.

It Pays to Advertise

Although it took three years for an advertising firm to sell their idea, on April 8, 1865, New Orleans city council proposed the proposition to display advertising placards on street cars pulled by mules. This new form of advertising became the first in the United States to be used on streetcars. It proved to be highly successful and quickly spread throughout the country.

Free News Pamphlets

Another first for New Orleans in the area of transit was furnishing patrons with weekly or bi-weekly news pamphlets placed in holders secured to its cars' window stanchions.

Streetcar Mardi Gras Floats??

The only time in Carnival and Mardi Gras history that electric-lighted floats on streetcars took to the streets was 1899. The parade was a total flop.

Fare Boxes
Omnibuses and Mule-Drawn Trolleys

From the very beginning, fares collected on these two modes of travel required the rider to drop his money in a fare box at the front of the car. The motorman (driver) could see through the glass front of the fare box. If change was required, he would give it to the passenger by dropping the change into a gravity slot. When the fare was paid, entrance was made in the rear of the car.

This is probably as early a one-man, pay-as-you-enter operation one could hope to find in New Orleans.

Exact Change

Yes, it is true-the old saying that "nothing is new, it's all happened before." In the case of exact fare as it exists today, this was par for the course at various times during the history of New Orleans transit.

When the September 4, 1874, Battle of Liberty Place that took place on Canal Street ended, streetcars that were used as fortifications were uprighted. Upon doing so, the transit companies found money still in the exact-change boxes.

Free Ride Thing of the Past

For many years, nuns, letter carriers with pouches, and policemen and firemen in uniforms were carried free. Detectives dressed in "civies" rode free by displaying a badge.

All Transit Consolidated

In 1922, all transit lines in the city were about to become consolidated. Under Louisiana state law, NOPSI was chartered to operate not only all transit service, but all electric and gas services as well. The official date was August 18, 1922. For the first month, the company was without a president. On September 27, Mrs. R. S. Hecht was elected the company's first president. One of NOPSI's first actions was very popular. Transit fares were reduced from 8¢ to 7¢. The popular new fare lasted 38 years.

In 1923, an extensive report was prepared by the J. A. Beeler Company of New York to help point out and also solve some of the transit problems. Beeler was effective in both areas. Their efforts led to banner ridership. By 1926, 148 million passengers rode over NOPSI's 26 street railway lines and five motor bus lines. During their studies, the Beeler report also uncovered some unusual findings. The report stated, "If the capacity loads carried by the cars of the New Orleans Railway and Light Company after 9:00 p.m. and through the night and thereafter are criterions by which the experts are to be guided, the people of New Orleans are human bats, as the street traffic in New Orleans is different in this respect from any other city in the United States. Another peculiarity of streetcar travel in New Orleans is that of Mondays. There appears no difference in volume between Saturdays and Mondays. One is as heavy as the other. This is due largely to the fact that all the big Canal Street department stores had their bargain day on Monday.''

Private Car on Streetcar Line
Yes, if you have the bread (money), you can always get that little extra-special treatment. New Orleans' railway system offered those with the financial ability three private cars for special occasions such as the opera and theater parties. The three plushly decorated cars' names were ''Sancho Pablo'', ''Atlanta'', and ''Palestine''. Rental cost was $15 per night.

CANAL STREET

Today, when flying out of New Orleans on a commercial airliner, chances are you will wind up going through Atlanta, regardless of your destination. Some years ago, when going to Las Vegas on vacation, my party was scheduled to fly out of

New Orleans on an aircraft which developed mechanical problems, and—you guessed it—we were rerouted through Atlanta.

Streetcar passengers in New Orleans had almost the same type of experience every time they rode on a streetcar. It seems that no matter where you were going, the streetcar either left Canal Street or rolled down Canal Street some time during its run.

At one time, during rush hour, Canal Street was literally solid with streetcars.

ELEVATED RAILWAY?

On March 27, 1882, New Orleans City Council passed an ordinance granting Thomas L. Airey the privilege of erecting an elevated railway along the riverfront adjacent to the French Quarter. Mr. Airey, prior to getting the okay to build this project, stated he was confident that once the line was put into operation it would be so successful the city would want to extend it to run along the entire riverfront of the growing city of New Orleans.

Although the ordinance was passed, Mr. Airey proved to be more talk than action, for the elevated railroad was never built.

If the proposed railway had been built, it would have been interesting to see how the good-natured, safety-first, old-reliable mules would have reacted to working at this new height. Chances are, the mules would have reacted like the mules in the following Mardi Gras story.

"JACKASS REBELLION"

For over 100 years, all Carnival and Mardi Gras parade floats were pulled by mules. For most of those years, they were sanitation department mules who pulled garbage wagons in the daytime, and, during Carnival and Mardi Gras, they pulled floats at night.

Over the years, a relatively small number of Carnival and Mardi Gras parades have been cancelled because of war, rain, fog, police strikes and political unrest. The most unusual cancellation ever was as follows:

Now mules might not be the brightest animals on God's green earth, but enough is enough even for the lowly mule.

After a full day at the office (pulling garbage wagons, that is), mules were brought to the parade staging area and immediately hooked up to the floats. The normal drab white cloth coverings were placed over the mules' bodies and then, and only then, were they fed.

In short order, it was time to get the parade on the road. The captain blew his whistle with great gusto, signaling it was time to move out.

But, as though they had just returned from a union meeting where they had voted not to pull the floats, every mule would not and could not be coaxed into moving. No matter how the handlers tried to get them to move, every mule held its ground, resulting in the parade being cancelled.

The incident was reported in the newspaper in bold letters as the famous "New Orleans Jackass Rebellion".

RENT STREETCAR FOR PARTY NOT NEW

As early as 1893, New Orleanians were able to rent a streetcar to hold birthday parties or other special events. Some who rented them stated they did so just to make whoopee. Prior to electric fans and air conditioning, this was an excellent way to beat the heat in the summer.

The transit companies promoted this type of entertainment for the populace. They would go out of their way to decorate the streetcars with colored lights to make the outing more festive. Things then were apparently as they are today, for there were those who wrote indignant letters to the newspaper editors asking the noisy party goers on rails to use the parks or private buildings where they would not disturb others.

No matter what you do, there will always be those who will be opposed to everything, including motherhood, apple pie and the American flag.

BUSES
RUBBER TIRED MONSTER

Just as the popular steamboats were ultimately replaced by steam-operated railroads that moved on steel wheels, steel-wheeled streetcars began their decline with the entrance of rubber-tired buses. They were called by streetcar lovers "rubber-tired monsters". The first public transit buses began operating in 1910. By 1929, the older-style engine-driven buses were replaced by electric buses, labeled "trackless trolleys". In time, the electric buses were replaced by diesel engine-driven buses.

Today, mini buses that are made to look like streetcars still travel through the center of the French Quarter. The larger buses operate only on the outer edges of the Quarter and throughout the city.

TYPES OF PROPULSION
THROUGH THE YEARS

Animal (horses and mules) 1831
Steam 1832
Walking Car 1866
Compressed Air 1868
Overhead Cable 1870
Ammonia Gas . . . . 1871 and 1886
Thermo-Specific (condensed steam, fireless) 1871
Electric Third Rail (public exhibit only) 1885
Electric Overhead Trolley (public exhibit only) 1885
Storage Battery 1889
Overhead Trolley 1893
Gas and Diesel Buses 1910
Electric Buses 1929

TRANSIT RATES OVER THE YEARS

1893	5 cents
1918	6 cents
1920	8 cents
1922	7 cents
1960	10 cents
1970	15 cents
1971	25 cents
1972	30 cents
1980	40 cents plus 5 cents for a transfer
1985	60 cents plus 5 cents for a transfer
1992	$1.00 (St. Charles Streetcar)
1992	$1.25 (River Front Streetcar)

TRANSIT STATISTICS

Year	Population	Passengers Carried
1840	102,193	N/A
1850	116,375	N/A
1861	170,000	N/A
1870	191,418	N/A
1880	216,090	23,716,327
1890	242,039	30,510,662
1900	287,104	53,184,273
1910	339,075	80,408,085
1915	364,000	83,184,938
1920	387,219	109,927,440
1924	422,000	145,156,000
1925	430,000	145,676,056
1926	435,000	148,488,286
1929	450,000	96,898,277
1930	458,762	116,207,798
1935	474,000	102,000,000
1940	494,537	124,000,000
1945	520,000	246,668,635
1950	570,445	216,817,236
1960	627,525	164,075,000
1970	593,471	Statistics not available.
1980	557,927	Statistics not available.

FIRST STEAMBOAT TO ARRIVE IN NEW ORLEANS

STERNWHEELER OR SIDEWHEELER?

The first steamboat to arrive in New Orleans anchored alongside the levee adjacent to the French Quarter on January 12, 1812. The ship was appropriately named "New Orleans". Since the plan was for the ship to carry freight and passengers from New Orleans to ports to the north, the name selection made good business sense.

Early ships were built without benefit of drawings. The customer would just make an outline on a piece of paper or sometimes in the dirt floor at the shipyard. The builders would start work, building according to what he was shown by the buyer. The workers were most capable. Building a major ship without benefit of a drawing took seasoned craftsmen with great skills. The lack of drawings for the ship leaves us 180 years later still befuddled as to whether she was a sternwheeler or sidewheeler. Writers of the day did very little to help clear up the confusion. Some described the ship as a sternwheeler, while others wrote of her as a sidewheeler.

There may still be confusion as to what she was in the method of propulsion, but there is no doubt of the economic impact the steamboat had on Louisiana and especially the French Quarter.

Chances are we will never know what type of propulsion the Steamboat New Orleans had. On July 13, 1814, the historic vessel hit a submerged stump near Baton Rouge. In trying to break loose from the stump, she took on water and sank to the bottom of the river. She might be gone, but the controversy as to her propulsion design is still with us.

SMOKEY MARY

The first railroad to begin operations west of the Alleghenies was the Pontchartrain railroad. The five-mile line operated on Elysian Fields Avenue between the Mississippi River and the community of Milneberg located on Lake Pontchartrain. The idea of this new mode of transportation for New Orleans was first discussed in 1825. In 1829, talk turned into action with the formation of the New Orleans Railroad Society. It was the first such society in America. It was also successful in carrying out its goal of a railroad line in New Orleans. On January 20, 1830, the Louisiana legislature incorporated the Pontchartrain Railroad Company. The New Orleans "Daily Picayune" reported "the ax was driven into the first tree March 10, 1830." The task of construction was not an easy one, for there were swamps and marshes between the river and the lake. To president M. W. Hoffman and engineer General Swift, the swamp and marshes proved to be only challenges, and in time were overcome. On April 23, 1831, a large crowd gathered to

witness the first run. Sometimes the best-laid plans of mice and men do go asunder. The locomotive ordered from Great Britain did not arrive for the dedication of the line. This was overcome by using six horses to pull each of the six cars. The first car carried General Governor Andre Roman and other state officials. The second, city officials. The third, a band. The fourth, railroad directors. The last two cars carried stockholders. In spite of celebrating without a steam engine, the celebration was a huge success as all who took part let off plenty of steam during the day-long event.

On June 15, 1830, the steam locomotive, affectionately called "Shields", arrived by steamboat. It was built by Mr. John Shields of Cincinnati. He wished he hadn't, for he was left with egg on his face when the engine proved to be totally unsuccessful. Later that year, a British firm, Rothwell Hicks and Rothwell, built a locomotive they called "Pontchartrain" since it was for the Pontchartrain Railroad. It arrived and was tested on September 6, 1832. It was only partially successful. It lacked enough power to pull the heavy load of passengers and freight. To augment the needed power, sails were added. This had to be quite a sight. Can you imagine seeing a steam locomotive coming down

the rails partially powered by sails. When the service began, the one-way fare to Milneberg from New Orleans was 37½¢. Round trip was 75¢. As usage increased, cost of operations went down and so did the fare. In the 1850s, it was reduced to 25¢ and later cut again to 20¢ with children under 12 paying 10¢.

The name that was affectionately used during its 100 plus years of existence was "Smokey Mary". The name was derived in the early years when all cars were open-roofed. This led to the passengers being covered with soot carried by the smoke as the train moved forward. Even though covered coaches became the norm, the name Smokey Mary stuck just as the soot had stuck on the early passengers.

Because of the Pontchartrain Railroad, New Orleans not only had the first railroad society, but also had the first freight-loading platform in America, and the world. All railroads up until that time had been loaded and unloaded in the manner that wagons had been loaded, by hand and/or hand cranes. The man credited with this ingenious idea, copied by all railroads around the world, was superintendent Captain Grant.

Another ingenious invention first used on this line was the safety device called the cow catcher. Since the track ran through grazing land for cattle, from time to time the engine and cars were derailed when a cow got in the way and the engineer was not able to stop in time.

Milneberg was truly a popular place on weekends. This fact is born out in that seven trips per day were made Monday through Saturday and nine were necessary on Sunday. The lakefront resort was usually packed to capacity every weekend. At some of the hotels and saloons, some of those who had a little too much to drink became rowdy and were taken into custody. Since there was no jail at Milneberg, the railroad would park a boxcar with barred windows on the siding. When someone was arrested, he was thrown into the makeshift jail. On Sunday night on the last run, the boxcar was brought back to town and a paddy wagon would be waiting to take the offenders to their final destination, the city jail.

CHAPTER THREE

CITIES OF THE DEAD

INTRODUCTION

After a short stay in New Orleans, you will realize it is unique in many ways. Therefore, it should not be surprising that its cemeteries are no exception. In fact, many of the city's stranger features are to be found in its cemeteries. One aspect that is not as noticeable as massive tombs and "wall ovens" is the large number of cemeteries within the metropolitan area. Almost every major city has a few large facilities. Not New Orleans. The "cities of the dead" now number 40 (not counting the ones that once existed). Like the city's many ethnic neighborhoods, its cemeteries are the same. They are scattered throughout the area and are ethnic in scope. Our being a close-knit community is borne out by the fact cities of the dead border up against residencies of those who are still alive. Just as the living reside in quarters crammed against each other, so are those who reside in the cemeteries. Both live in harmony with absolutely no complaints from one group, and only once in a great while a complaint from a recent resident of the other. Those who do complain, we know, don't reside within the confines of the cemetery. We also know that those within the walls care little or pay no attention to those who complain.

Although space does not allow stories from all 40 cemeteries, the following will give you a good example of the uniqueness of New Orleans' cities of the dead.

ST. VINCENT DE PAUL
GYPSY FUNERAL LONG REMEMBERED

In 1832, a new cemetery was established at 1322 Louisa Street. Records do not acknowledge who specifically, or what company, began the cemetery, only that it was built by a priest. Apparently because of the street address, it became known as the Louisa Street Cemetery. In 1857, New Orleans' most-renowned duelist, Señor Pépé Yulla, purchased the cemetery and ran it along with his other business enterprises. Some claim that he not only owned and operated it, but, with proficiency of every weapon used in dueling, he helped on many occasions to fill it with those who had the audacity and poor judgment to challenge him. As one man stated, "If he didn't fill the graveyard, he at least furnished it with a beginning any mother would have been proud of." Unlike many who participated in the deadly art of dueling, Señor Yulla died of old age (73) on November 11, 1888. This alone was testimony to his expertise as a duelist. As one would expect, he was laid to rest in what had come to be known as the Pépé Yulla Cemetery. The cemetery was operated by his family up until 1910, at which time it was sold to Albert L. Stewart.

St. Vincent de Paul Cemetery, the name by which it is known today, is famed as the last resting place of a noted gypsy queen. On November 9, 1916, people in all areas of the city learned by word of mouth that a fancy funeral parade, unlike any held before, was wandering merrily through the streets with the body of Marie, Queen of the Tinker Gypsies. With New Orleanians' love of parades, it wasn't long before the streets were lined on both sides with men, women and children. It was more like a Mardi Gras parade than a funeral procession. The mourners, both those on foot and those who followed in a long line of colorfully decorated carriages, were all dressed in bright gypsy costumes. When they were not playing their tambourines, dancing, and munching on grapes, they were drinking wine. It was joviality from start to finish of the long parade that serpentined its way to the cemetery. Once the colorful, noisy group reached the cemetery, they went directly to a large tomb that had been built to receive Marie's body. While the queen's body was being placed within the tomb, singing and dancing continued. When the body was entombed and the opening sealed, each member of the Tinker Gypsy tribe made impressions, using coins of many nations, in the soft cement. This part of the ceremony completed, each man and woman in the group, with a full bottle of wine in hand, approached the tomb, sprinkled wine on it, and what was left they drank until the bottle was empty. After all had completed this step, they left in silence.

This was by no means the end of the celebration. It was only a period for the living to recharge their batteries for the next celebration that was to take place. When the tribe arrived the next day, they brought with them long tables, which were set up in front of the tomb. When in place, they were loaded down with foods of every description, along with wine and grapes. When the feast was completed, masons put a second coat of cement over the first. When this task was completed, certain members of the tribe, apparently royalty, using their rings,

made impressions in the soft cement. After the last impression was made, a marble slab was placed over the opening. As a finale, the grapes that remained were thrown against the tomb, and a lighted candle was placed in a black receptacle. Only then did the members of the tribe depart in silence.

For many years, the sexton could tell every time a member of the Tinker tribe passed through New Orleans. He would notice a lighted candle and grapes on and about the tomb.

The sexton was rather confused in 1937 when a gypsy approached him and demanded the marble slab be removed. Not wishing a confrontation, he did what was asked of him. The gypsy, seeing the ring impressions, was satisfied the queen's remains had not been disturbed, and told the sexton to replace the slab. When the slab was in place, he took wine and grapes from a bag he was carrying and performed the usual rite, including lighting a candle. The only difference, once the candle was lit, the gypsy did not leave. Instead, he turned to the sexton and requested that on November 9th each year, he, the sexton, perform the wine-grapes-and-lighted-candle rite. To show his gratitude, the gypsy told the sexton he would, each year, send the two bottles of wine and grapes needed for the ceremony, plus an extra bottle of wine for his troubles. The gypsy then told the sexton he had traveled over 10,000 miles to check the tomb and perform the ritual. The reason he gave: the gypsy queen, Marie, was his loving mother. For many years, on November 9th, as promised, grapes and wine arrived. The sexton, moved by the gypsy son's request, graciously carried out his wishes, and, of course, consumed the bottles of wine sent for that purpose.

METAIRIE

John Erskine, a famous author and world traveler, once wrote after his visit to Metairie Cemetery, "It recalled his visit to Pére la Chaise Cemetery in Paris, but was far more beautiful." Having visited and studied both, I am also convinced Metairie Cemetery is not only the more beautiful, but is far more historical, as well. A few examples to substantiate this statement are as follows:

TEMPLE OF ATHENA NIKE'

Metairie Cemetery is the location of hundreds of magnificent monuments dedicated to those who have gone before us. One such striking tomb is the final resting place of William G. Helis, an international oil magnate, a native of Greece, who came to New Orleans to make his mark upon the world. His love of his native land is evident in his final resting place. His mausoleum, designed by the noted Ralph Phillippi, is a scale model of the classical Temple of Athena Nike' which is located on the Acropolis in Athens.

His monument is not only beautiful but unique. In his will, Mr. Helis stipulated that he be buried in the soil of his native land. To carry out his final wishes, one of his numerous ships was sent to Greece for sufficient quantity of Greek soil to be transported back to New Orleans and placed in Metairie Cemetery beneath the replica of the classical Temple of Athena Nike', Mr. William G. Helis' final resting place.

PYRAMID

Even though Egypt is thousands of miles from New Orleans, Egyptian architecture is to be found in Metairie Cemetery in the form of a pyramid. It is located not too far from the Greek temple described above. The pyramid is the final resting place of Lucien Brunswig, who had been head of a

local wholesale drug firm. The Brunswig family was from Germany. After seeing the original tomb in the largest cemetery in Munich, they decided this would be their choice for their final resting place. It is a true pyramid. At the entrance is a grilled bronze gate. Flanked to one side is a beautiful, yet weatherworn marble sphinx. On the other, a female figure, with one hand pointing to the name above the entrance and the other holding an urn. Through the years, the weather played havoc with the fingers on both hands. Being stone, there is no way she could have gotten nervous and bitten her nails.

Pyramids are known to give out a mystic aura. That may account for the direct lightning strike that damaged the structure. True, there are many taller tombs and monuments in the area of the pyramid, but they were spared. The pyramid took the direct hit. The upper stones were moved and damaged. Fortunately, the larger apex stone was not disturbed. Necessary repairs were made and the structure was put back in first-class condition. You could say it is now electrifying to look at. The area where the pyramid is located, because of the large number of massive expensive tombs, is called Millionaires' Circle.

CELTIC CROSS

From the earliest period of Christianity in Ireland, crosses were engraved on standing stone slabs. This proved to be the easiest means of Christianizing the ancient pagan cult of the standing stone. From this tradition evolved the impressive freestanding crosses of stone that are such a distinctive feature of Celtic/Christian culture. On the Holy Isle of Iona off the coast of Scotland, massive carved Celtic stone crosses guard the graves of 40 Scottish kings, including Macbeth, the same Macbeth who was made famous by the writings of Shakespeare.

With the enormous influx of Irish immigrants to New Orleans in the early nineteenth century, it was inevitable that the Celtic crosses would eventually top the graves of proud Irishmen who made this city their home.

One of many magnificent examples of the Celtic cross can be found in Metairie Cemetery. This majestic 18-foot, 15-ton monument is the Palfrey-Rogers-Brewster Celtic cross. The carvings that are found on all faces and sides were done only after careful historical research. The carvings are rich in symbolism with deep religious overtones.

In the near future, another massive Celtic cross will reach

toward the sky over New Orleans. This one will not be for a famous king, not even a Mardi Gras king, or a prominent family. This cross will stand and serve as a reminder of the 8,000 poor, and, in most cases, uneducated, Irish immigrants who died in the 1830s while digging the New Basin Canal through the fever-infested swamp between the present Union Station and Lake Pontchartrain. The park where the cross is erected is appropriately located directly over the former waterway that became the final resting place of many of the brave Irish immigrants.

ANGELE MARIE LANGLES
105 LA. 39

Metairie Cemetery in New Orleans is the location of a 30-foot Egyptian obelisk. There is no flowery epitaph to the deceased nor are the remains of the deceased below the beautiful monument. The simple inscription chiseled on the base of the cenotaph (a monument erected in honor of a deceased whose remains are elsewhere) reads, "Angele Marie Langles 105 La. 39". The inscription may be simple but the reason for the inscription, on the other hand, is far from simple. It came about because of a court case involving a conflict of last wills and testaments.

In 1898, Angele Langles and her mother, Pauline Costa Langles, well-to-do New Orleanians, made necessary travel arrangements for a trip to France by way of the French steamer LaBourgoyne. Both ladies made wills favoring each other before departing. On July 4, 1898, two days out of the Port of New York, the LaBourgoyne sank, with a loss of more than 500 lives, the Langles among them. Angele, the daughter, in her will called for the erection of a monument for herself. Her heirs protested. Since the wills of both women involved different sets of heirs, the courts were called upon to decide which of them had died first. The preliminaries of the case started out in a New Orleans courtroom in the Presbytere. From there it went to the Louisiana Supreme Court. The decision of the Louisiana Supreme Court was as follows: The daughter, being younger, was presumed to have survived the mother. (Ironically, those who

knew the Langles family were aware of the fact that the daughter was frail and the mother had a strong constitution). The Supreme Court ordered that a sum of $3,000 from Angele's estate be spent in erecting a cenotaph in her memory. The executor instructed her name and the legal reference to the case be engraved on the monument. With this information, all who

passed and wished to learn the circumstances under which the memorial was erected could read the opinion of the Supreme Court of Louisiana that ordered its erection.

TALLEST PRIVATELY OWNED
MONUMENT IN U.S.
NO PROBLEM
ONLY A CHALLENGE

In the early 1900s, Daniel Moriarty decided, as an act of love, to order a massive granite monument for his deceased wife, Mary Farrell Moriarty. In dealing with the architect, he stipulated that the monument had to be the tallest privately owned monument in the United States. When the drawings

were completed, its design showed the monument would stand sixty feet tall. A circular plot eighty-five feet in diameter was purchased in Metairie Cemetery. Super salesman Daniel Moriarty convinced the owner of a Barre, Vermont, quarry that if they offered him a special price for the monument, he could help them dominate the very profitable memorial industry in New Orleans.

When the monument arrived, there wasn't a drayage company that could handle it. Persuasive Daniel, with his silver tongue, overcame the obstacle by convincing the Illinois Central Railroad to lay a spur track from Carrollton Avenue along the New Basin Canal to the edge of the cemetery.

The monument was delivered and erected, proving that there is no challenge too great to overcome when expressing an act of love is involved.

MAILHES-KRAUSS

The Mailhes-Krauss Memorial is one of the most distinctive monuments in the cemetery. No doubt the family believed the old saying, "the only thing worse than not being able to read is to be able and not read." Stretching 20 feet across the rear of

the plot is a roll of books carved from a solid block of granite. In the middle are six closed volumes representing the elders of the family. The three larger books have the names and dates of the husbands, while the shorter volumes list the wives. The open volumes to the right and left of the closed volumes are ready for the next generation. The idea for this unique memorial was that of Marjorie Herbert Mailhes.

BYZANTINE CHAPEL
WITH BELL

Augustus Bernau was the principal orator at the laying of the original entrance lodge of the cemetery. When his wife Elizabeth died, Mr. Bernau had a small Byzantine chapel erected as her burial place. The simple dignity of its outside is in marked contrast to the beauty of the inside, including the ornate marble and alabaster altar. Mr. Bernau had the builder install a bronze bell in the domed cupola. From the bell extended a chain that descended into the tomb. The interesting story about the bell and chain is as follows: Mrs. Bernau was fearful that she would be buried alive. With the chain in hand, if that did happen, she would have a second chance by ringing the bell to gain attention. The story also had been told that, during the summer months when there are a number of grass cutters working in the cemetery, some pranksters would ring the bell and then watch and laugh as the workers headed posthaste for the nearest exits. No doubt, where there were no exits, new ones were made. One other unique feature of this tomb is found inscribed in the rear of the tomb. Still quite legible is a long epitaph and excerpt from the speech Mr. Bernau delivered at the dedication.

LOTTERY KING

Not only is Metairie the last resting place for a number of Mardi Gras kings, it is also the home of the man who became king of the original Louisiana lottery. His name was Dr. Maximillian A. Dauphin. Although he was not the founder, he was without question the brains behind its unbelievable success. When he took over the reigns, he hired two heroes of the Confederacy, Generals P.G.T. Beauregard and Jubal Early. This was done to prove, without a doubt, its honesty. The daily and weekly drawings were affordable for the average citizen, but the larger pots for the monthly drawing were out of reach for a large portion of the population. To overcome this obstacle, Dauphin devised a scheme of splitting tickets for the monthly drawing so that all could afford to take part in the drawings.

On the front of the tomb is a tall baroque pylon of granite with the name Dauphin in large letters. The entrance into the tomb is by way of a huge granite door located in the rear. In-

scribed on the door is the name M. A. Dauphin M.D. and the date.

There is a strange oddity to be found on this tomb. Facing the front, as you walk around to the left side, upon reaching midway, located parallel to the ground on the base, you will find a cutout in the granite. You can lift the plug and chances are you will find some coins. It has been said that, if you play the lottery, good luck will be yours by putting a few coins under the cutout before you place the bet.

GATES OF PRAYER
LIGHTHOUSE!!!

    Chances are that of the hundreds of thousands who pass the Gates of Prayer Cemetery in the 4800 block of Canal Street, few, if any, have noticed the replica of a lighthouse in the center of the cemetery. It was placed there in memory of Harry Offner, founder of Harry's Hardware. He was a major supporter of the Lighthouse for the Blind and worked diligently in helping the visually handicapped find a means of livelihood.

ST. JOSEPH NO. 1

St. Joseph Cemetery No. 1 does not have the beauty or history of Metairie or the history of St. Louis No. 1. The residents within were mostly hard-working, fun-loving everyday people who lived from one day to the next. They may not have large impressive tombs, and none, you can rest assured, were from the social register. What they did have was something most of the other cemeteries did not. St. Joseph No. 1 has the original St. Mary's Assumption Church. When con-

structed in 1844, it seated only 80 people. By 1860, the parish outgrew the little church. A larger and grander building was constructed, and the smaller structure was moved to its present location inside the cemetery. It is one of the oldest structures in uptown New Orleans.

ST. LOUIS NO. 1
VOODOO QUEEN
1796 - 1881

Although the tomb of Marie Laveau, the last known witch of North America, is not as massive, ornate or architecturally renowned as many others in the cemetery, it is visited by more people from all over the world than any other tomb in the cemetery. Marie Laveau was the illegitimate mulatto daughter of a wealthy white plantation owner named Charles Laveau. As a member of the Louisiana legislature, he had many influential friends, leading to great wealth and power.

Marie was a very beautiful young woman. She married Jacques Paris, a free man of color. When Jacques died, Marie took up with her lover named Glapion. Marie gave birth to 15 children. It seemed like someone might have been putting a curse on her. In order to support her family, she became a hairdresser.

She was extremely good at her chosen trade. In no time, her clients were the creme de la creme of New Orleans society. In doing the hair of the beautiful ladies, she found that they not only let their hair down, but also confided their innermost feelings.

Marie, like all citizens of the city both black and white, knew of the popular practice of voodoo. The practice was brought to New Orleans and North America by the slaves from Africa and Haiti. Because Louisiana law allowed only Catholicism, all slaves born in Louisiana were baptized Catholic. But because slaves had deep religious roots in voodoo, they combined the two religions. In time, they worshipped the Catholic Virgin Mary alongside the snakes of the voodoo doctors.

No doubt, with the genes of a Louisiana politician as part of her makeup, she found she could make far more money selling

voodoo potions to her clients than what she charged them for doing their hair. In fact, she gambled in the beginning by charging
10 times as much as others in the trade. The higher price in itself,
she believed, showed how good she really was. To guarantee she
would sell the right potions to achieve the ultimate goal, she had
people she knew that would report back to her, hired as domestic
help in the households of her largest and most prosperous clients.
Once she worked for a well-to-do couple whose son had serious
legal problems. Marie, with some of her purported magic, meaning her close alliance with judges, was able to work wonders in
this particular case. Even though the young man was found guil-
ty, the judge acquitted him. Marie came out smelling like a rose
in this instance. The young man's father was so grateful, he gave
Marie a house on St. Ann Street.

Marie was number one in her voodoo trade, having no close
rivals. She lived in luxury to the ripe old age of 98.

Today she is still number one. Hers is the most-visited tomb,
not only in St. Louis No. 1, but of all the city's cemeteries.

The standard tradition when visiting Marie's tomb is to
place a single "x" on the white-washed tomb if you wish for
something, and a double "x" if you wish for something bad to
happen to someone else. It seems that it has always been the
case that wishing misfortune for others is more popular than
wishing something good for ourselves. Marie's tomb is covered
mostly with double x's.

ST. LOUIS NO. 2
ALEXANDER MILNE

True, you can't take it with you, but Alexander Milne, a philanthropic Scot found a way to let everyone know where it did go. Milne was an immensely successful businessman. During his time, he owned more than 20 miles of land along the shores of Lake Pontchartrain. Before he passed away in 1838 (age 94), he devised a scheme to let the world know what happened to his wealth. He specified in his will that the entire contents of his estate be imperishably engraved on his ornate monument.

Milne, no doubt, knew what he was talking about when he said "imperishably engraved", for the engraving is as legible today as it was 155 years ago when it was inscribed.

GIROD STREET

Christ Episcopal Church, the first non-Catholic church in New Orleans, was founded in 1805. The congregation decided almost immediately there was a definite need for a burial facility for their deceased. The only cemetery in the city at the time was the Catholic burial ground, St. Louis Cemetery No. 1. It was a Catholic owned and operated facility which allowed only Catholic burials in the main area. All other denominations and those without religion were buried in the rear, outside of a wall. Behind this second section was yet another area, set aside specifically for black citizens.

The religious congregation of Christ Episcopal Church organized a number of committees, including a burial committee. Their goal was to obtain the small burial plot behind the walled burial section of St. Louis No. 1. In a relatively short time, their goal was achieved. In fact, the newly founded congregation had a burial ground before they had a church. All went well for one and one-half decades. In 1820, out of the blue, the city fathers asked the church to relinquish the property. The reason given: the city needed the land for a street to satisfy the needs of the growing population. The congregation once again found itself without a place to bury its dead. Without delay, another cemetery search committee was formed. This time, they went after a larger piece of ground to help satisfy the burial needs of the ever-growing number of parishioners, as well as the increasing city population in general. They felt that this would allow burial not only for their own flock but also a burial place for others. This would allow them to generate income necessary to achieve their religious goals. Finances were a problem, so they looked at land on the outskirts of town. The plot they had their eye on was in a very low area. It had the appropriate nickname, "The Swamp". The area was susceptible to flooding during both light and heavy rains. In time, the nickname proved to be most accurate. Even though the area was not the best, the cost, like the property, was also low. $3,140.67 was the asking price for the 3-1/2 acres. This they considered affordable and fair. The rectangular square of land was surrounded by Girod, St. Paul (now South

Liberty Street), Perrilliat and Cypress Streets. The second factor for the bargain price was the close proximity to a large number of honky-tonks. These establishments were so rowdy and dangerous, police did not go into the area after sunset, and only in large numbers during daylight hours. To sell the property in this area for residential purposes would take a super salesman. None even tried.

On August 10, 1822, the property was purchased when the

city council authorized Mayor Joseph Roffignac to sell the described property located in Faubourg St. Mary to Christ Episcopal Church. To help them purchase the unappealing property, the city allowed payment over a ten-year period. They considered the sale a godsend.

Girod Street Cemetery, unlike St. Louis No. 1, was laid out in an orderly fashion. There was a wide center aisle and two side aisles. These were bisected by 22 cross aisles. The walls surrounding the grounds, like St. Louis No. 1, were used for what came to be known as "wall ovens", because of their similar

look to the bakers' ovens in use at the time. The wall ovens were massive and had a burial capacity of 2,319. Because of the low elevation, unlike St. Louis Cemetery No. 1, virtually all burials were meant to be above ground.

The first to be buried in the consecrated ground were the remains of those parishioners (who were previously treated as second class citizens) who had been buried behind the wall of the St. Louis No. 1 Cemetery.

In time, Girod Street Cemetery became the final resting place of political leaders and military heroes, such as Colonel

William Wallace Smith Bliss. Bliss was a hero in the Mexican War, and the person for whom Fort Bliss, Texas, is named. Within the walls were also multitudes of business tycoons and renowned entertainers. One of the city's medical giants was Dr. Dow. Prior to his demise, he left in his will he wanted a skull and crossbones carved in his monument. Although a strange request for a doctor, his wish was carried out.

John David Fink, one could say, believed in the old saying, "I may forgive, but I will never forget." He was a German immigrant who chose New Orleans as his adopted home. He was a sturdy specimen of a man, living to the ripe old age of 70. Back in his youth, he had fallen in love with a girl who hurt his feelings by laughing at his suit. She wanted, she said, to work out her own destiny. Old Mr. Fink, at the end of his life, showed himself to be a charitable man, leaving a large sum for protestant widows and orphans. He decreed that it was to admit no old maids. "Let them", he said in his will, "work out their own destiny."

Lieutenant Charles F. Fuller, killed during the mutiny on his ship, the "San Antonio", while she lay at anchor in New

Orleans, was laid to rest in the Protestant cemetery. A number of the crew members were tried, sentenced and executed for their parts in the mutiny. Not only were they buried in the same cemetery, but not far from Lieutenant Fuller.

SOCIETY TOMBS

In the 1800s, benevolent societies were very popular throughout the city. "Society tombs", as they were called, were especially popular in this cemetery. Benevolent societies predated insurance companies. Every ethnic group had a society which collected a small fee from their members weekly. Membership assured medical attention when needed and proper burial in the end. There were well over 100 benevolent society tombs. Each contained anywhere from 12 to 70 vaults. Some of the more imposing tombs rose to as many as eight tiers above the ground. In the 1850s, a visitor wrote of these tombs:

"The largest and finest tombs in the Protestant cemetery (public or society tombs) are those owned and erected by slaves. The 'ovens' contained a large number of slaves; for anyone who has money enough to pay for an oven can be deposited in this cemetery whether black or white, bond or free. The cost of burial in the ovens or in the vaults of the society tombs is about twenty dollars. This is sometimes paid by the slave and very frequently by the master. The slaves have, however, by means of the principle of association, erected fine monuments and tombs of their own. The following societies of slaves owned their own tombs: 'The First African Baptist Association,' 'The Home Missionary Benevolent Society,' 'Male and Female Lutheran Benevolent Society.' This last society was a tomb containing upwards to 70 vaults—a very elegant and costly edifice, entirely above ground."

Some of the society tombs bore fanciful names. The invention of their African American owners. Among them were "Wide Awake Benevolent Society," "Ladies of Labor Benevolent Association No. 2," "United Sons of Honor Association," "St. Mary Tabernacle No. 6," "Morning Star Tabernacle No. 2," "Pure in Heart Temple No. 1," "Young and True Friends Benevolent Association." As late as 1904, these groups were still building tombs in Girod Street Cemetery.

The most impressive of the "society" tombs in the Girod Street Cemetery was built by the New Lusitanos Benevolent Association. This massive tomb was really a mausoleum with a

row of vaults on each side of a covered corridor. The portico was done in marble and granite, with two substantial Doric columns ornamenting the facade.

The Lusitanos tomb was the property of the New Lusitanos Benevolent Association, a colorful group founded on September 11, 1858, as a mutual benevolent society. Six hundred strong, the association adopted as its motto "We nurse the sick, bury the dead, and protect the widows and orphans." Despite the name, the membership was drawn from people of several national origins other than the Portuguese. There were Germans, British, Irish, French, etc.

The renowned architect for this beautiful tomb was J. N. B. de Pouilly. Some believed it to be the largest in the city when built. It had a spacious interior, with 100 small vaults, and was 30 feet front and 30 feet deep with a walk five feet all around. The entire structure was enclosed by an iron railing. In October of 1859, construction of the tomb was complete. Cost of this eye-catching addition to the cemetery was $6,000.00. When they were ready to dedicate their new burial place, what better way than with a parade! And what a parade it turned out to be. Members of the New Lusitanians met in full regalia, which included colorful, rich blue scarves and rosettes. There was not one, but three divisions, each with a band. The mayor of New Orleans, recorders and city councilmen all took part. Starting at 10 o'clock, the procession marched down Front Levee Street to the corner of Barracks and Old Levee Streets, where an American flag was presented to the association by Ms. Sara Hoggarth. From there, the procession proceeded down Chartres Street to St. Ann, around Jackson Square, where a salute was fired. When the procession reached St. Louis and Toulouse Streets, they stopped to receive a flag which was presented to the association by its French members. On to Chartres to Camp, then to Lafayette Square where yet another salute was fired. They marched down St. Charles Street until they reached Girod. There they marched to the Girod Street Cemetery to inaugurate their new tomb. Once they reached the cemetery, another salute was fired, and an address was given by Anthony Sambola, secretary of the association. When he completed his delivery, yet another salute was fired. From there they went up Julia to Carondelet, in Canal to Royal, down Royal to Esplanade, Levee, Engheim, Greatmen to Elysian Fields where a "token" was presented to Mrs. Inez Barcelow, Godmother of the association's Banner, then up Frenchmen to Washington Square, where, you guessed it, another salute was fired. By the time the members left Washington Square, their ears were ringing and their tongues had to be hanging out, but this did not discourage them. They proceeded to the Third District Exchange, where refreshments were served, and they listened to yet another address. This one was delivered by E. Morel, a member of the association. When they had had something to eat and drink and caught their second wind, the procession reformed again. Yes, they were weary, but the marchers were still standing erect and proud as they walked down Love to Rampart and St. Ann Streets to their hall, where they disbanded.

FIRST NIGHT TIME
FUNERAL PARADE?

From the earliest days of New Orleans, funeral parades were a common sight. Military funerals with their pomp and ceremony were colorful and impressive.

With the birth of the Protestant Girod Street Cemetery came a new spectacle in funeral parades. One such parade was described by the editor of the "Daily Orleanian":

"It was the first night funeral ever witnessed, we believed, in New Orleans; and, as the well disciplined

Montgomeries, with measured pace, moved slowly along, to the roll of muffled drums, through the gloom-wrapped streets, their tall plumes nodding at each tramp, and their arms, in contra-distinction to the Gen'l. Scott order, solemnly reversed, crowds wonderingly gazed on them and the almost spectral scene presented, so dim and unearthly did it appear.

"The sun's last crimsoning hues had vanished from the clouds ere the cortege took up its line of march from Esplanade Street; yet notwithstanding the coming darkness, the martinet soldier in command never permitted a quick step, but slowly and reverently paced along. On reaching the Girod Street Cemetery, so still and calm was the hour, that, save the heavy and regular tramp of the military, and the re-echoings, through the church yard, of the low, quiet strains of the 'Dead March from Saul,' nought else broke on the ear. Even the city's busy hum was hushed—hushed as the unbroken and eternal sleep of the mouldering defunct around. When the funeral discharges were fired over the grave of the buried, bat and owl, disturbed from their reveries, took to wing and flew alarmingly about. It was a scene to firmly impress itself on memory's page."

YELLOW FEVER MOUND

In the early years of the 19th century up until the Civil War, New Orleans was considered a commercial center. Those who came, with a little luck, could and did make fortunes in incredibly short times. People with this in mind flocked to the Crescent City from all over the world. Unfortunately, the city was, in a sense, a two-headed dragon. Cholera and yellow fever stood guard before the gates of plenty. Many of those who came to obtain their fortunes and bury their menial past, wound up being buried in Girod Street Cemetery. Many became victims of epidemics which plagued the city on numerous occasions. From 1796 on, the city was a victim almost annually of the epidemics of sicknesses which were transported to New Orleans through its commerce with the islands of the West Indies, Cuba and Mexico. In 1832, the city was visited by a devastating cholera epidemic. Dr. Michel Halphen, a French physician who practiced in New Orleans, wrote of it:

"Never in any country has cholera shown itself so terribly. Six thousand died in 20 days-about one sixth of the population of 35,000 that had remained in the city. The accumulation of bodies at the cemeteries was so great and disorder and confusion so bad that graves were opened at random to make room for new bodies. Finally, it became necessary to dig large trenches, and in them the coffins were laid five deep with scarcely two feet of earth thrown on top of them. Quicklime was used over the coffins, but it was scarce and of such poor quality so the effect was almost null. Many bodies were brought to the levee, bricks attached to the feet, and then thrown into the Mississippi to be rid of them."

A New Orleans street scene during the yellow fever epidemic of 1853.

Reverend Dr.. Theodore Clapp described the conditions in his autobiographical sketches and recollections during a 35-year residence in New Orleans. He wrote:

"Many persons, even of fortune and popularity, died in their beds without aid, unnoticed and unknown and lay there for days unburied. In almost every house might be seen the sick, the dying and the dead. All the stores, banks and places of business were closed. There was no means, no instruments for carrying on the ordinary affairs of business; for all the drays, carts, carriages, hand and common wheelbarrows, as well as hearses, were employed in the transportation of corpses instead of cotton, sugar and passengers. Words cannot describe my sensation when I first beheld the awful sight of corpses driven to the graveyard and there upturned, and their contents discharged as so many loads of lumber or offal, without a single mark of mourning or respect because the exigency rendered it impossible.

"Often I was kept in the burying grounds for hours in succession by the incessant unintermittent arrival of corpses over whom I was requested to perform a short service. One day I did not leave the cemetery until nine o'clock at night; the last interments were made by candlelight. Reaching my house faint, exhausted, horror-stricken, I found my family all sobbing and weeping for they had concluded from my long absence that I was certainly dead.

"One morning...at six o'clock I stepped into a carriage to accommodate a funeral procession to the cemetery. On my arrival, I found at the graveyard, a large pile of corpses without coffins, in horizontal

layers, one above the other, like corded wood. I was told that there were more than 100 bodies deposited there. They had been brought by unknown persons, at different hours since nine o'clock the evening previous. Large trenches were dug, into which these uncoffined corpses were thrown indiscriminately."

This area in the cemetery was traditionally called "the

yellow fever mound'' (many of the city's cemeteries had such a mound). No tombs or monuments were built in this area which measured roughly 40 feet by 100 feet. In one of the great epidemics, the space had been used for mass burials. Even though records of interment kept by the sextons go back to 1835, nowhere is there an entry or a clue as to the date of the mass burials in this site. It is true there were great epidemics in 1832, 1847, 1853, 1854, 1855, 1858, 1867 and 1878; during none of these years is mention made of mass burials. If a guess had to be made, it would be the great cholera epidemic of 1832-1833.

When the decision was made to close the cemetery in 1957, the "yellow fever mound" was excavated to a depth of five feet (since mass burials were made in shallow trenches), and all remains found were reinterred in Hope Mausoleum on Canal Street.

DEATH OF THE FACILITY
FINAL NAIL IN THE COFFIN

Unfortunately, the cemetery was not an architecturally imposing place of last rest. True, it was well laid out with a wide central aisle and fairly regular side aisles, but somehow, despite several imposing tombs erected in it, Girod lacked the character of the newer Cypress Grove or the contemporary St. Louis Cemeteries on North Claiborne Avenue. Rain caused flooding to the point that the sexton, at times, could be seen rowing around the cemetery in a skiff carrying a coffin. The Girod

Streetcar Line that brought people to the front entrance went out of existence. Hoboes and bums in large numbers took up residency; many resided in the larger tombs. The quietness of the cemetery was in complete contrast to the drinking establishments, railroads and warehouses within close proximity. People, as already stated, unfortunately neglected upkeep of the tombs.

G-P LINE

Another cause of the demise of the Girod Street Cemetery, besides neglect, being lowland and surrounded by noisy industry and rowdy drinking establishments, was its difficulty in being reached. There was only one streetcar line that went to the cemetery. It was called the Girod-Poydras (G-P) line. Someone jokingly said G-P stood for "Get out and Push". Unfortunately, its tracks were so bad the passengers, it was said, couldn't tell if the car was on the rails or bobbing along the cobblestones in the street. The Picayune newspaper was quoted as saying, "the Girod Street line had no'good days', except perhaps on All Saints Day, and then the traffic was confined to a very few people, who, out of sheer curiosity, visited the city of the dead".

In time, complete tombs were covered with overgrowth,

while others were totally destroyed by tree trunks. Vandals got into the cemetery and stole everything that was resellable. The first items to go were wrought iron, marble slabs and statues. Thieves broke open over 1,000 vaults to steal the gold from the teeth of those within. When the cemetery's income dwindled, so did the sexton's pay. His take home pay was so low, he was required to supplement his income by raising chickens in the cemetery. The entire cemetery became an eyesore and embarrassment to Christ Episcopal Church and the city. Things had gotten so bad, they literally could get no worse.

After World War II, the City of New Orleans was humming with activity. Just as the city had purchased the land from behind the old St. Louis No. 1 Cemetery, Christ Episcopal Church, because of need of a new street, they were once again approaching Christ Episcopal Church in hopes of purchasing the Girod Street Cemetery, with the purpose of widening streets. The federal government, at the same time, needed a

piece of property for a new post office. It was decided by the hierarchy of the church that the property would be sold, the cemetery deconsecrated and the remains of the 22,000 interred be removed.

A monumental task was undertaken to notify families of the need to make plans to remove the remains of their loved ones. A small percentage of families responded. While this was being done, preservationists did what they could to preserve the most-outstanding vault slabs which were left. Because of the unbelievable vandalism, only 13 distinguishable slabs remained. These were removed and attached to the rear wall of the Canal Street wing of Hope Mausoleum in St. John Cemetery. Members of the Louisiana State Museum removed the few pieces of statuary and carvings which had survived the

onslaught of vandalism. These are now at the Louisiana State Museum (Cabildo). When what was salvageable had been removed, work of demolishing the tombs and vaults began. In all, an estimated three million bricks were taken from the grounds during demolition.

During removal of the remains from the tombs, hundreds of saucers and plates were discovered. These, it is said, were placed on the chests of the deceased at wakes of poor families. As friends paid their last respects, they dropped in an offering to help defray the cost of the burial. The money was removed before burial, but the saucers were placed in the coffins with the bodies.

DECONSECRATED

On January 4, 1957, the cemetery was officially "deconsecrated" by the Rt. Reverend Girault M. Jones, Bishop of Louisiana. By March 8, 1957, the monumental task

of removing the 22,000 bodies was accomplished. Those remains that were not claimed by the families of the white citizens were reinterred in Hope Mausoleum. Those of the Negro dead were removed to Providence Memorial Park. Two memorial tablets in Hope Mausoleum commemorate the event. A bronze tablet at the memorial park marks the spot where the mass reinterments of the black citizens were made.

$3,140.67 TO $332,708.00

The approximate 3-1/2 acres of land purchased in 1822 by Christ Episcopal Church for $3,140.67 was sold in 1957 for $332,708.00. The federal government's share was $294,000.00. They bought the bulk of the land, which was used as a site for the garage for the post office. The city paid $37,683.58 for the necessary land to widen streets in the area.

CHANGING TIMES

Where 22,000 once lay motionless in rest, today hundreds of thousands of automobiles, trucks, motorcycles and pedestrians move back and forth like ants. For 135 years, within the walls of the cemetery 22,000 souls were quietly laid to rest. Today, the federal post office no doubt has that many letters in their dead letter file.

DEAD BUT STILL ON THE MOVE

It is somewhat ironic that those who died in the 1800s were still moving in the 1900s. Those interred into the rear of the St. Louis Cemetery in the early 1800s were moved to the Girod Street Cemetery. After 135 more years, they were once again moved, this time to Hope Mausoleum and Providence Memorial Park.

THREE DIFFERENT NAMES

It is also ironic that Christ Episcopal Church has had two cemeteries and both were deconsecrated to make way for streets necessary to handle a growing population. Let us hope that the remains of those who have been moved twice since their deaths lie in their present location for all eternity.

The Girod Street Cemetery was also known by the majority of New Orleanians as the Protestant Cemetery. We say majority, for the only name used by the Creoles was Cimetire des Herétiques. From that name, we can surmise there was no love lost between the two factions.

GOING IN STYLE

In the mid 1800s, an innovative New Orleans entrepreneur came up with a novel idea that paid off handsomely. Fancy wakes, with magnificent coffins and plush surroundings, followed by burial in an impressive tomb, were fashionable. Those without the necessary finances were envious of those who could afford such a splendid way of making their final exit.

Mr. Entrepreneur said to himself, "Now here is a need involving large numbers of people; how can I satisfy this need?" While in deep thought, as though a bright light went on in his head, he said, "Ah, ah, I think I have found the solution. I will be able to supply those with meager means with a magnificent mahogany coffin with plush silk lining and monstrous silver

handles. The burial will be one of the most impressive monuments to be found within our city." His idea was accepted and purchased by many who wished to go out in style. Wakes were attended by many of their friends, who saw them in the mahogany coffins and then buried in a massive monument. They were duly impressed. What they did not know was what they had seen was available to the deceased for only 72 hours. After that time, the mahogany coffin was secretly removed from the massive monument, and the remains of the deceased were placed in a plain, unfinished coffin and placed in a simple grave.

NEW ORLEANS CEMETERY LOCATIONS

St. Louis No. 1...Basin and St. Louis Streets
St. Louis No. 2...North Claiborne Avenue, between St. Louis and Iberville
St. Louis No. 3...3421 Esplanade Avenue
St. Patrick No. 1, No. 2, No. 3...143 City Park Avenue
St. Roch No. 1, No. 2...1725 St. Roch Avenue
Lafayette No. 1...1427 Sixth Street
Lafayette No. 2...Washington Avenue, between Loyola and Saratoga
St. Joseph No. 1, No. 2...2220 Washington Avenue
St. John...4841 Canal Street
Metairie...5100 Pontchartrain Boulevard
Cypress Grove...120 City Park Avenue
Greenwood...5242 Canal Boulevard
Odd Fellows Rest...5055 Canal Street
St. Mary-Carrollton...Adams Street, between Spruce and Cohn
Carrollton...Adams Street, between Hickory and Birch
St. Bartholomew...Algiers
St. Mary...Algiers
Masonic...400 City Park Avenue
Holt...635 City Park Avenue
St. Vincent de Paul No. 1, No. 2, No. 3...1322 Louisa Street
Valence Street...Valence Street, between Danneel and Saratoga
St. Vincent-Soniat Street No. 1, No. 2...1950 Soniat Street
Gates of Prayer No. 1 (Beth Israel)...4800 block Canal Street
Gates of Prayer No. 2...Joseph Street, between Pitt and Garfield

Hebrew Rest...2003 Pelopidas Street

Dispersed of Judah...4901 Canal Street

Ahavas Sholem...Elysian Fields, Stephen Girard, Frenchmen and Mandolin Streets

Anshe Sfard...Elysian Fields, Frenchmen, Stephen Girard and Mandolin Streets

Jewish Burial Rites...Elysian Fields, Frenchmen, Stephen Girard and Mandolin Streets

Charity Hospital...5050 Canal Street

Mt. Olivet...4000 Norman Mayer Avenue

Beth Israel...Stephen Girard, Elysian Fields, Frenchmen and Mandolin Streets

Chevra Thilim (formerly Temmeme Derech)...South Anthony Street, near Canal

CHAPTER FOUR

PICTORIAL
THEN AND NOW

INTRODUCTION

Over the past 276 years, the architectural face of the Big Easy has, as would be expected, changed. Some areas have changed drastically, while other areas like the French Quarter have changed very little. The French Quarter looks almost exactly as it did after the 1788 and 1794 fires. When comparing French Quarter photos from the turn of the century and today, the only real differences in the area's appearance are the cobblestone streets, brick sidewalks, and old-time street light fixtures of the earlier years, which are no longer in existence.

Of all the different areas of the Big Easy, Canal Street seems to have changed more then any other street. Since its inception in the early 1800's, the look of Canal Street's neutral ground has been changed considerably every 25 to 30 years.

The one section of the city that has seen the most drastic change in the most recent years has been the riverfront, especially in the downtown and French Quarter areas. Up until recent times, a view of the river from street level was virtually impossible. The entire riverfront was used for docking ships. Massive warehouses, used to store the ships' cargoes, lined the riverfront. Where dilapidated warehouses once stood on the down-river side of Canal Street, today stands the Moonwalk, Woldenberg Park, and the sparkling Aquarium of the Americas turning a blighted area into a beehive of pedestrian activity. On the up-river side of Canal Street is located the city's largest hotel, the Hilton, the city's plushest condominiums, along with buildings left from the 1984 World's Fair. Today they serve as a shopping mall and other commercial uses.

Also covered in this pictorial chapter is the city's newest land mass. Beautiful Lake Vista was built from sand pumped in from Lake Pontchartrain in the late 1920's and early 30's. In number of years, the area is merely a baby in a city that proudly boasts of being 276 years old, yet has the vim, vigor, and vitality of a teenager. In one of those quirks of faith, Lake Vista is responsible for Lakeview no longer having a view of the lake.

Someone once stated that three things one cannot escape in his lifetime are death, taxes, and change. This chapter pictorially brings out the latter.

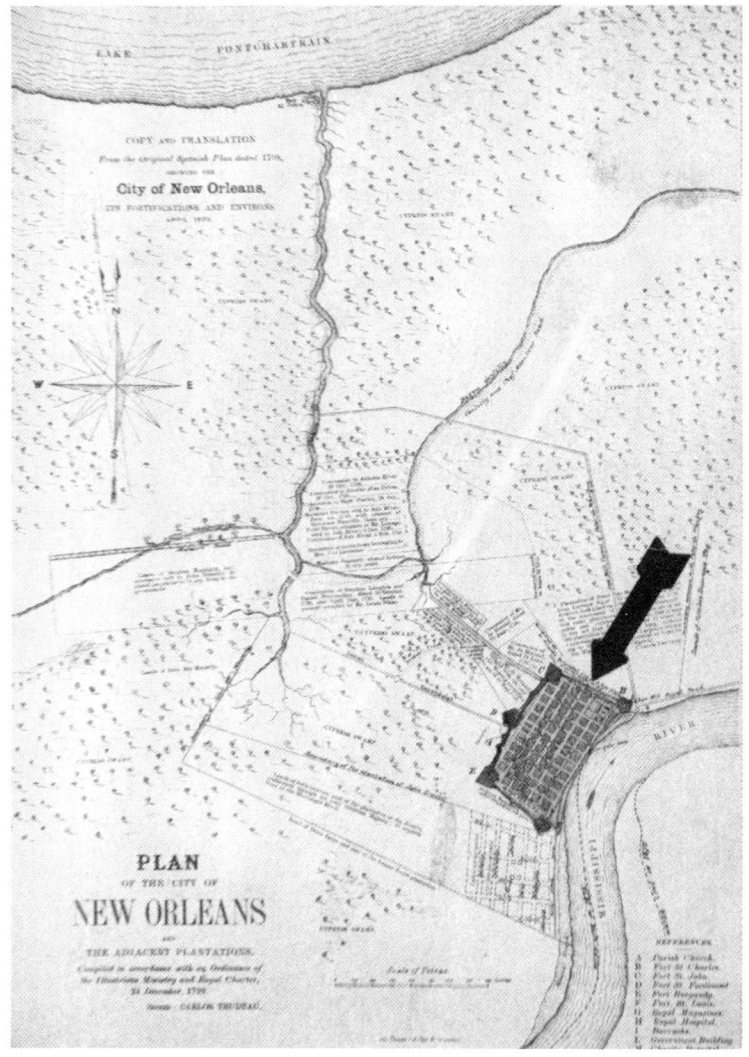

1798 Plan of the city of New Orleans. Arrows point to French Quarter.

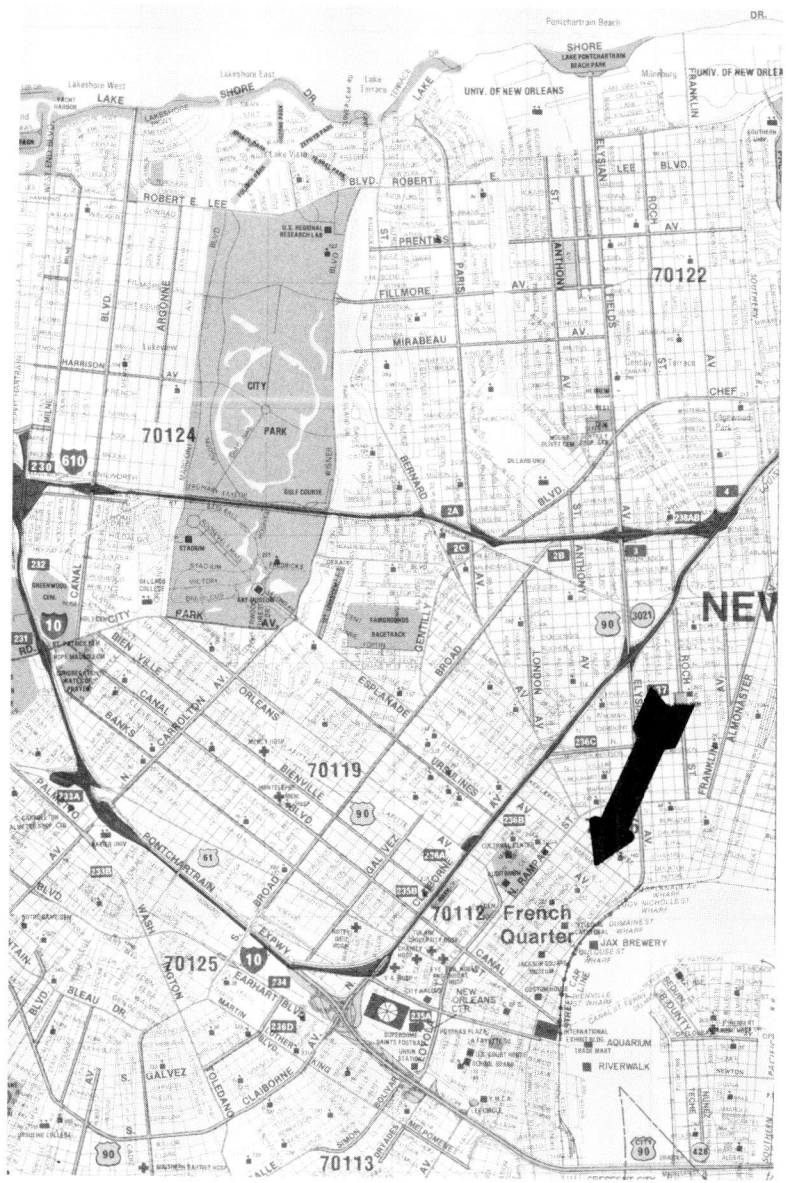

1852
New Orleans Harbor with its forest of masts and sooty cylinders. Arrows point to steeple of St. Louis Cathedral.

1867
View of postwar crowd at Metairie Race Course (now Metairie Cemetery)

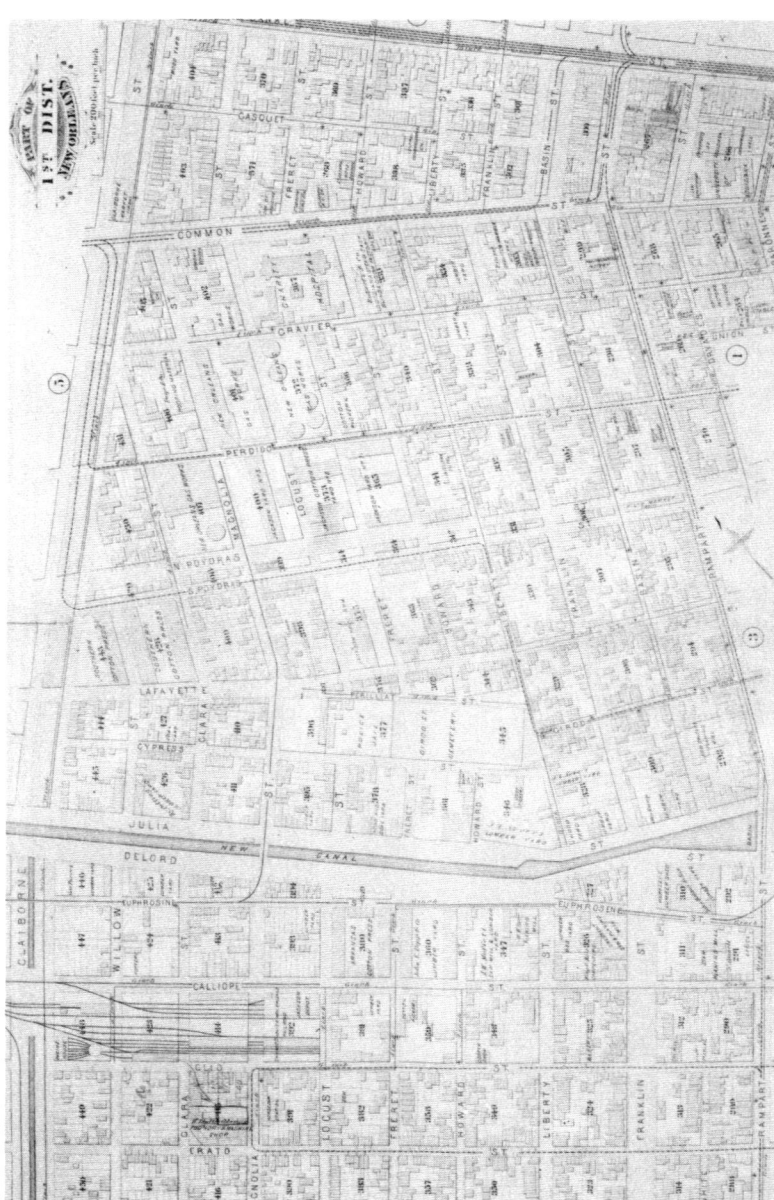

1884

Area bounded by South Claiborne, Perdido, Rampart, and Euphrosine was once location of a major canal-cemetery-jail-wood and coal yards-gas works-cotton presses-sawmill. Now the home of the Superdome, shopping center, office buildings, hotel, City Hall, train and bus terminal, and Interstate Highway.

1884

Audubon Park in 1884 was the site of the 1884 World Cotton and Industrial Centennial. The large building (see arrow) on the right was the main building of the fair. It covered 33 acres under one roof. Four present-day Louisiana Superdomes could fit in the area of that one building.

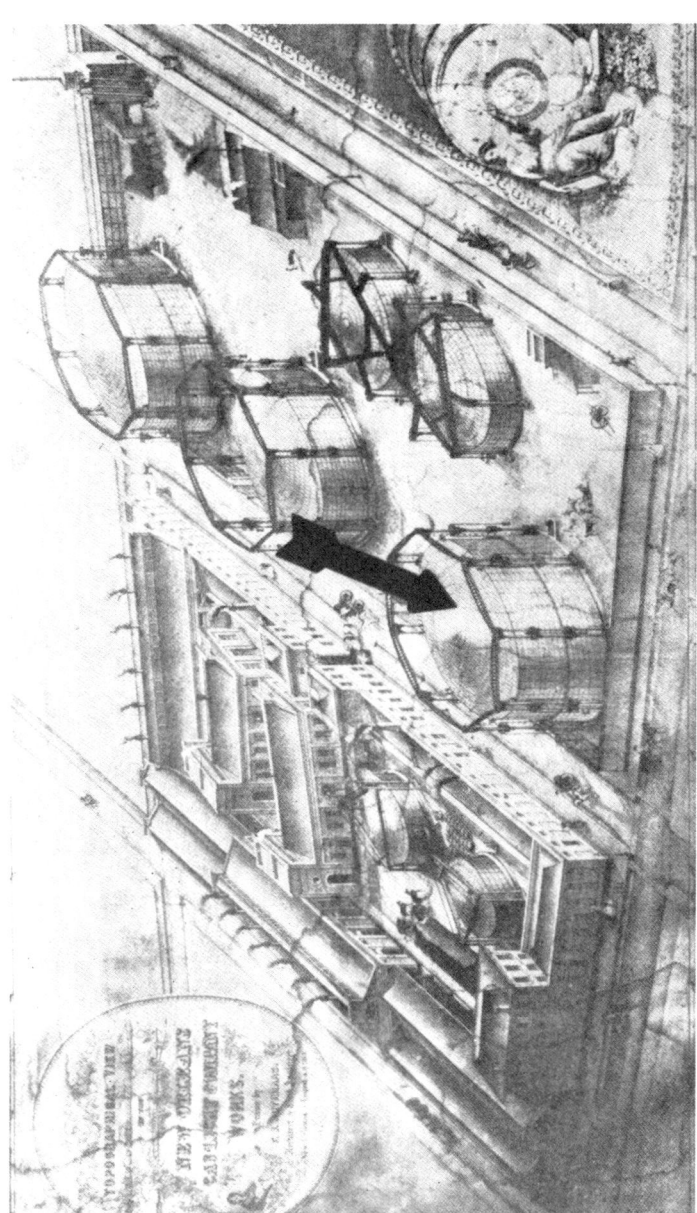

1884

The massive New Orleans Gas Works supplied gas to the entire city of New Orleans. It was located on Perdido Street. This is now the site of the VA Hospital. The metal tops of the tanks rose and fell depending on the pressure in the tanks.

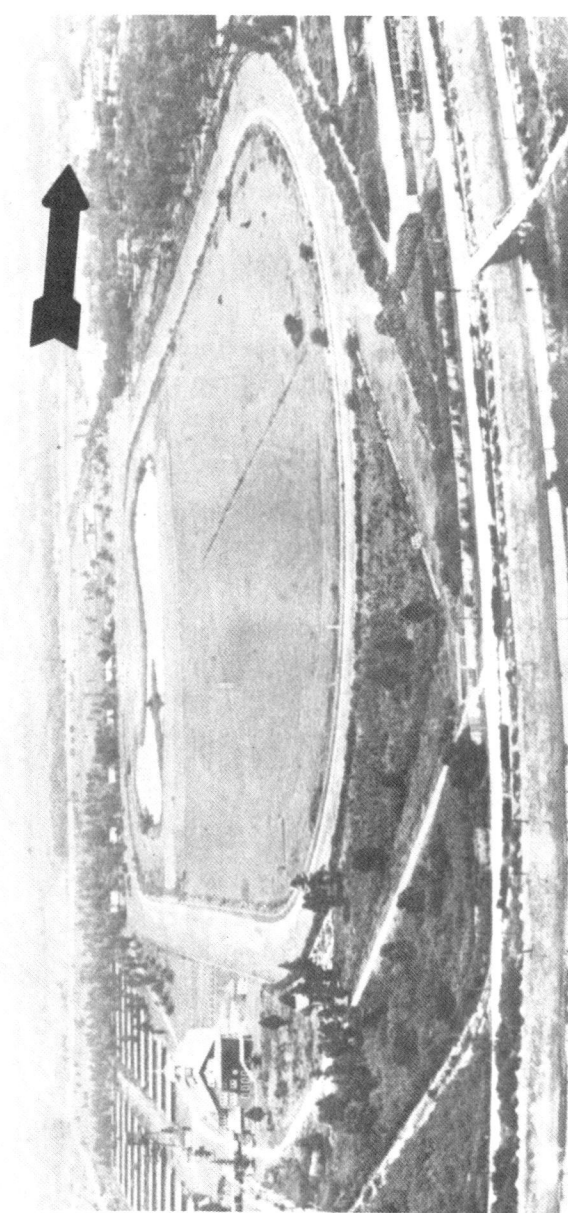

1913

The one-mile oval is City Park Race track. It began horse racing February 11, 1905. The street at the bottom of the photo is Marconi Drive. The building at upper right (see arrow) is the old Delgado Museum, renamed New Orleans Museum of Art.

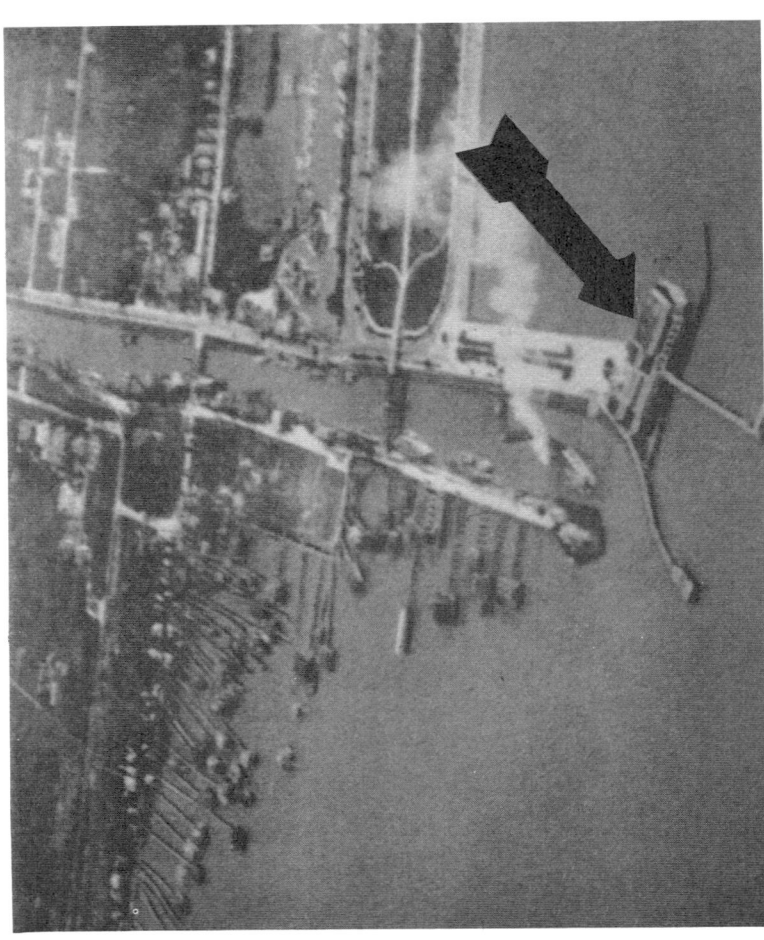

1920's
West End has been a place of fun and pleasure for the people of New Orleans since the early 1800's. The bottom of photo shows the Southern Yacht Club (see arrow), second oldest yacht club in America. The area to the bottom left where the camps are built out over the water is present-day Lake Vista.

1920's
Canal and Rampart Streets looking towards the River - Maison Blanche is tallest building on the left side of the street.

1920's
Canal and Rampart Streets looking towards the lake - building on right side of the street (arrow) was the Southern Railway Terminal Station. This structure was torn down in the early 1950's. Basin Street now occupies what was once S.R.T.S.

1920's

This aerial view was taken over Lafayette Square. The building on the right side of then City Hall, along with the First Presbyterian Church facing the square, and many other buildings have long been torn down. The tall structure is the Hibernia National Bank Building (see arrow) erected in 1920-21. It is 23 stories, 355 feet, in height, and was the city's tallest structure until after World War II.

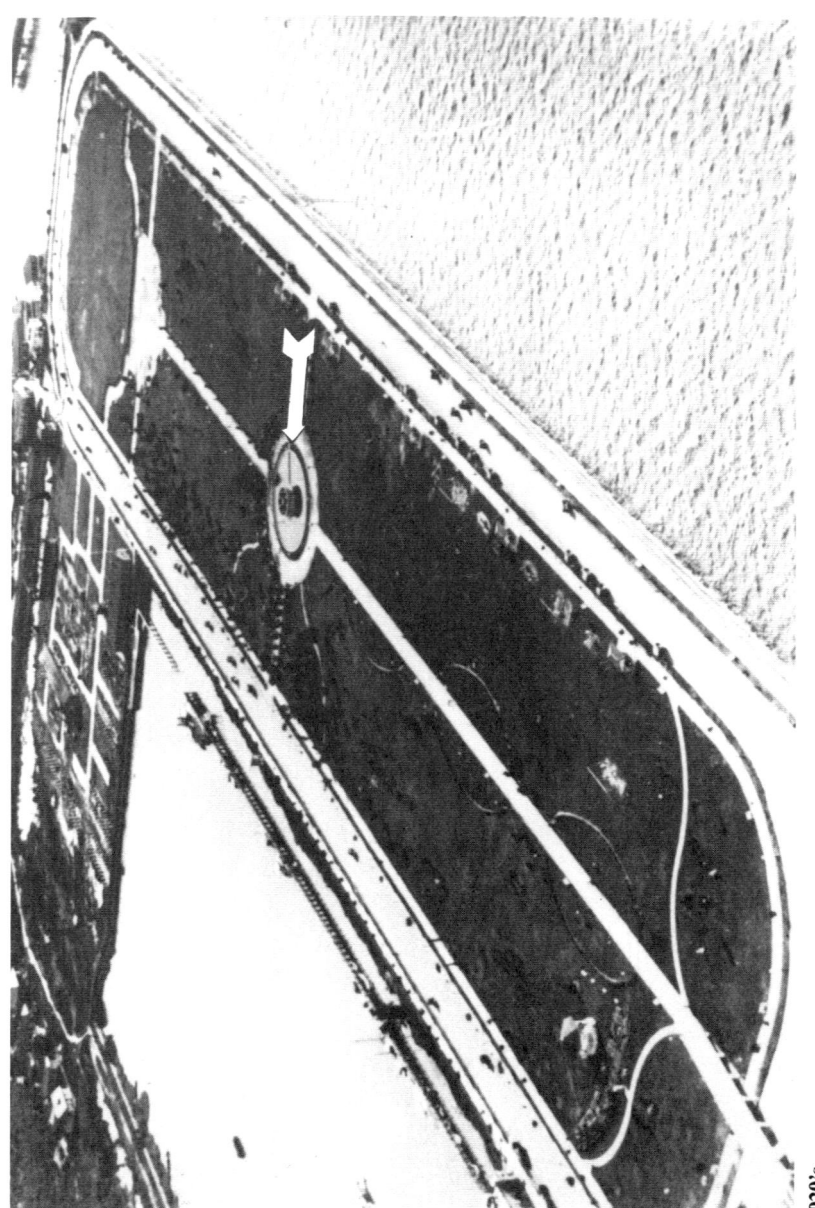

1920's
West End Yacht Harbor was so new there were no boats docked in the inner or outer harbors at that time. The circular object (see arrow), left center, is a large fountain.

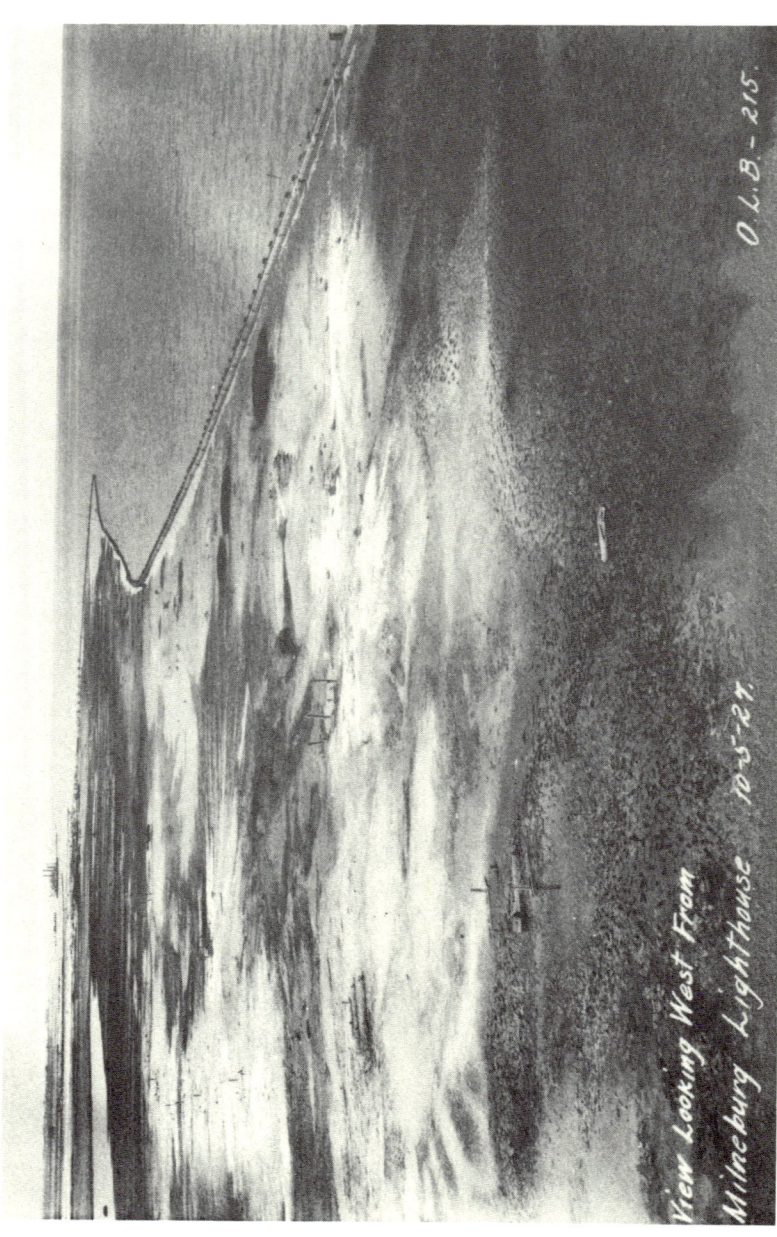

View Looking West From
Milneburg Lighthouse 10-5-27.

O.L.B. - 215.

1920's - 1930's.
Approximately one-half mile of Lake Pontchartrain was reclaimed to build present-day Lake Vista., Old Pontchartrain Beach and the UNO Campus. Prior to this project, present day Robert E. Lee Boulevard was adjacent to the lakefront.

1920's
St. Charles Street at Poydras Street looking towards Canal Street. Arrow points to famous old St. Charles Hotel, torn down and replaced by Place St. Charles building.

View Looking South from Milneburg Pier

1920's
The Lighthouse, dating back to 1839, was located at Milneberg (later the site of Pontchartrain Beach) and was originally more than one-half mile from land. The railroad tracks to the left formed the northern end of the line for the one-time Pontchartrain Railroad that ran from the Mississippi River to Lake Pontchartrain.

1930

Streetcar track construction at foot of Canal St, near the river. Photo taken on corner of Canal and South Peters Streets looking towards the river. A viaduct (see arrow) was and still is used by ferry passengers to cross the railroad tracks.

1930's

Bayou Metairie at one time flowed between Metairie Cemetery and Metairie Rd. The bayou at this location was filled in to widen Metairie Road and make it four lanes. See first picture in this chapter; shows Bayou Metairie in 1700's when it connected with Bayou St. John and Bayou Gentilly.

Date 8-15-4

1940's
During World War II the U.S. Government built the Michoud Facility to serve as a manufacturing plant to aid the war efforts. When completed, it was the largest building (see arrow) under one roof in the world. Today Martin Marietta builds the exterior fuel tanks for NASA's space shuttles.

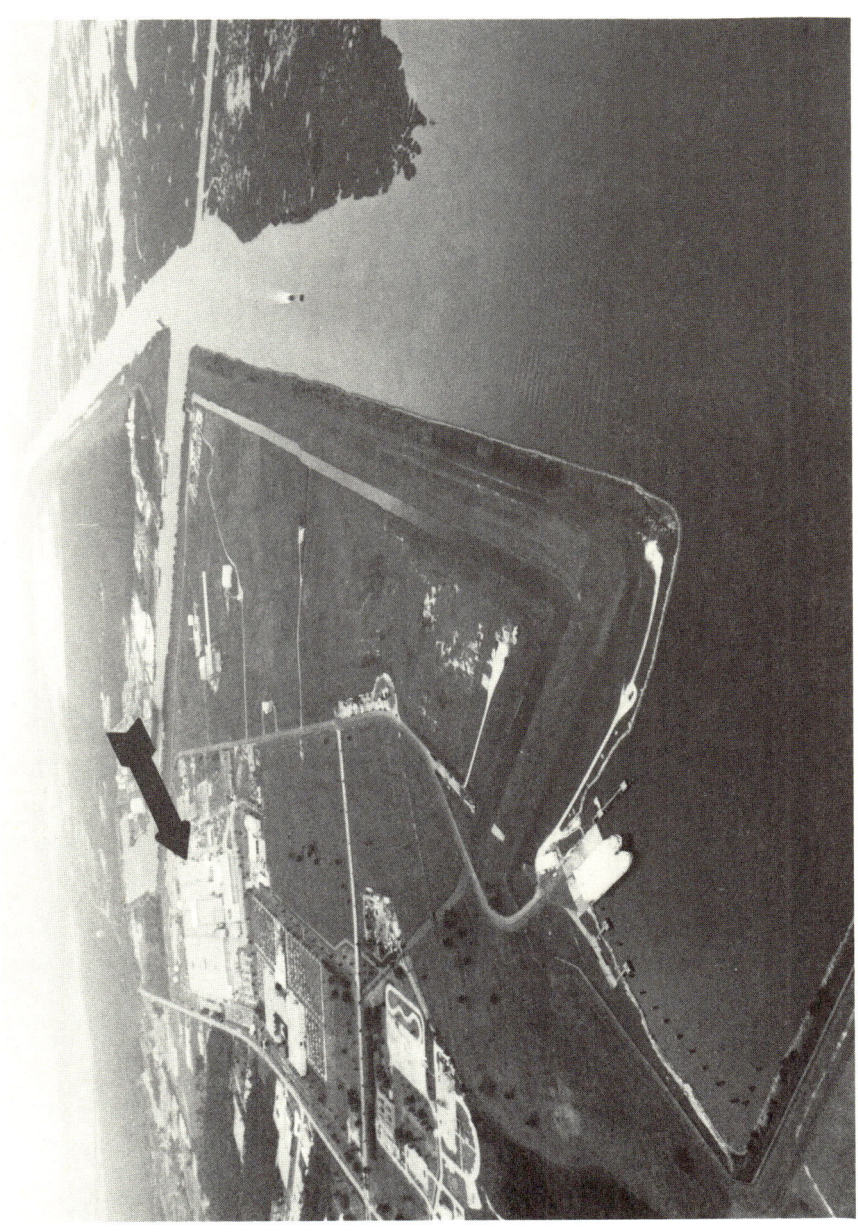

1942
Photo taken at intersection of Polk Avenue and Pontchartrain Expressway. Streetcar heading towards Lake Pontchartrain. New Basin Canal (left of streetcar tracks) ran from Rampart Street to Lake Pontchartrain - along route of today's Pontchartrain Expressway.

1955
Pelican Stadium (formerly Heinemann Park) located on the corner of Tulane and Carrollton Avenues. Demolished end of 1950's.

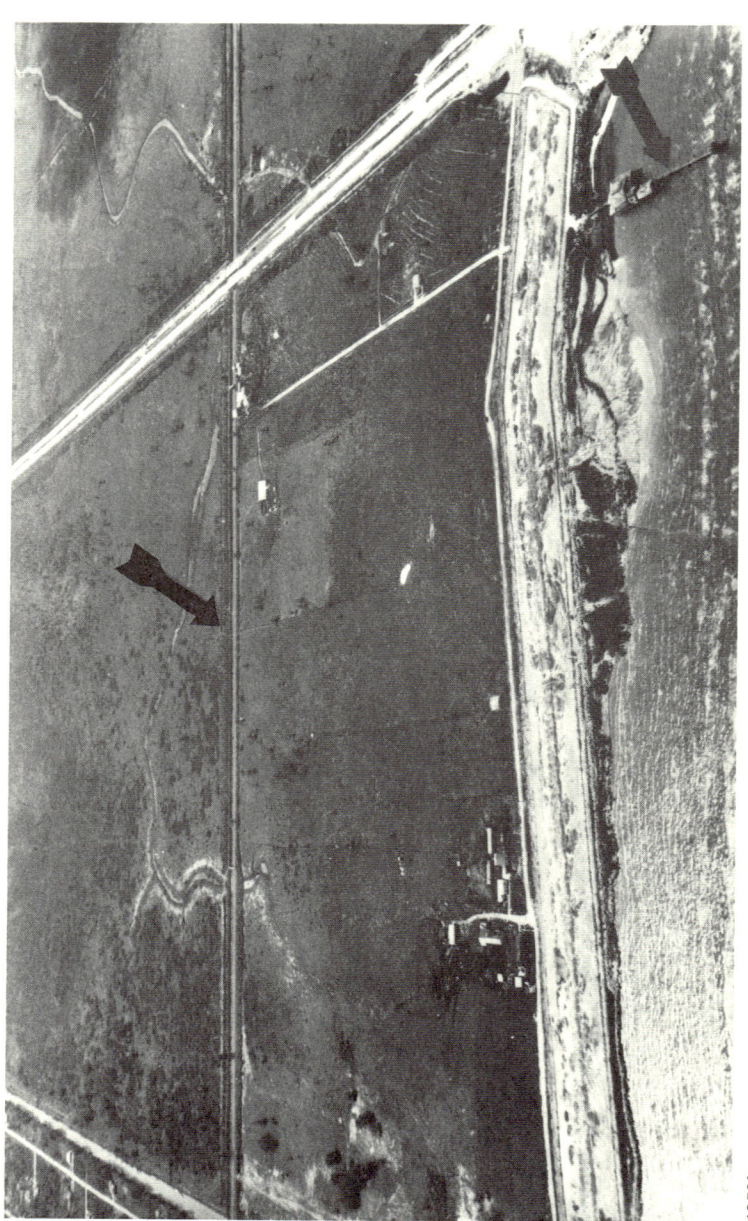

1950's

The Pontchartrain Causeway was well under construction when this photo was taken. To get ready for the onslaught of predicted traffic, Harlem Street was made into a four-lane artery and the name changed to Causeway Boulevard. The building over the water, bottom right (see arrows), was the Edgewater gambling casino. The canal running parallel to the lake in the middle of the photo (see arrow) is the West Esplanade Canal.

1950's
Greater New Orleans bridge (now Crescent City Connection) under construction. By tradition, the American flag was raised when the final piece of steel connecting both banks was put in place. Original span was completed in 1958.

1960's
Downtown skyline
What a big difference a few years can make! Louisiana Superdome opened August 3, 1975

CHAPTER FIVE

A MELANGE
OF
HISTORICAL FACTS

INTRODUCTION

This, the final historical chapter, is a collection of what I hope you will find to be interesting facts and drawings that fall into no category of their own, yet are important enough to be a part of the text.

The material covered could be called "Odds and Ends", "Bits and Pieces", or even "This and That". The reason the chapter is named "A Melange of Historical Facts" is because it sounds and appears to be the best description of the hodgepodge of material covered.

PHILIPPE DUC d'ORLEANS

The City of New Orleans was named in honor of Philippe Duc d'Orleans.

Upon the death of Louis XIV, better known as "The Sun King", his five-year old great-grandson son became heir to the throne. Because he was far too young to rule the country, his cousin Philippe Duc d'Orleans was made Regent—meaning he had absolute power in ruling the country. He served in this capacity from 1715 to 1723.

New Orleans was founded in the year 1718. John Law was the man who proposed the name New Orleans. His reasoning was strictly business. He was selling an important financial proposition to the Regent and was catering to his ego.

Visitors to New Orleans, because of the song "Way Down Yonder in New Orleans" (Or-Leans), are taken aback when they find out this is not the way it is pronounced by native Orleanians. They quickly learn that there are multiple pronunciations of the name.

NEW AW LINS
NEW OR LONS
NEW AW YONS
NEW OR LEENS
NEW AWL YONS
NEW OR LAY ON
NEW AWL LENS
NEW OIL LEENS
NEW OR LEANS
etc., etc., etc.

YOUR PRONUNCIATION NEW—

The one redeeming fact is, although there are many different ways to pronounce the city's name, there is no incorrect way.

FRENCH REVOLUTION
LED TO
FOOD EVOLUTION

The single most influential factor leading to New Orleans' rise to international prominence in the culinary arts came as a result of the French Revolution. In 1793, both Louis XVI and his lovely queen lost their heads to the guillotine. Before the revolution was over many noble families suffered the same fate. Every wealthy family had its own private chef with his small army of assistants and his treasured file of ingenious dishes for which he was famous. These private chefs, with so many aristocratic appetites lost to the guillotine, were forced to other less-proud pursuits. Many migrated to the little Paris of America, New Orleans, and either cooked for the wealthy or

Louis XVI

**A Gentleman
To The End.**

**Ladies First,
My Dear!**

opened restaurants. Here they found the same level of appreciation for their art as they had enjoyed in their homeland. To New Orleans these great chefs brought their secret recipes, the finesse of French sauces and subtlety of seasonings. They were captivated by the fact that the people of New Orleans lived to eat and did not simply eat to live.

GULLET SCIENCE

The proud Creoles who founded the city taught us how to enjoy many of the finer things of life. They enjoyed the opera, ballroom dancing, chamber music and many, many other niceties of life. They considered cooking the highest of the home arts. They called it "Gullet science" and their favorite expression was "An empty sack cannot stand alone." Through the years, food has been used for almost every important occasion from a small king cake for an intimate party at Mardi Gras, to a table buckling under the weight of a massive variety of foods that are first displayed and then consumed by an appreciative group of hungry people who attend a St. Joseph's Day altar.

LOCAL WEDDING CAKE TRADITION

Over the years many colorful traditions had their beginning in the French Quarter then spread throughout the city, sometimes throughout the country. One of these traditions is found at local weddings and goes as follows:

LOCAL WEDDING CAKE TRADITION

At wedding receptions, before the wedding cake is officially cut by the bride and groom, those bridesmaids who are single along with other single ladies at the reception each select the end of a silk ribbon that protrudes out of the base of the wedding cake. Baked into the cake are 12 small objects that are attached to the other end of the ribbon.

At a designated time the single ladies are given the signal to pull the silk ribbon to see what their fate will be, which is determined by the object on the end of the ribbon.

The following is what each of the 12 items represent.

Anchor — Hope   Horse — Sports
Clover — Good Luck   Silver Dime — Wealth
Fleur-de-lis — Flowery   Bull Dog — Tenacity

Button — Bachelor   Thimble — Old Maid
Horse Shoe — Good News   Wishbone — Success
Heart — Love   Wedding Ring — Matrimony

CREOLES LOVED THEIR COFFEE

Since the very beginning of the city's colorful history, locals have always had a passion for drinking coffee. The Creoles had a saying for almost everything. Regarding coffee, they said they liked it:

Black as the devil,
Strong as death,
Sweet as love,
And hot as hell!

As popular as the pastime was, it was not until March 17, 1930, when the managers of the Delta Steamship Company, then the Mississippi Shipping Company, introduced their employees to a daily 3:30 p.m. coffee recess. Company scouts had found the custom to be very well received in Brazil and adopted the idea for its New Orleans office. The tradition started by the shipping company spread like wildfire, which only goes to prove good news travels fast.

One last reference to coffee and chicory. A visitor from the North, upon tasting his first cup of coffee with chicory, said, "Wow! This Stuff is strong enough to get up and get its own sugar." Then he ordered another cup and a pound to go.

JASS/JASZ/JAZ/JAZZ

New Orleanians are proud that America's first art form was born in their city. Today it is called jazz. Although the music was born in the Crescent City, the name of the music was not. In 1916, a group of young New Orleans musicians were contracted by a Harry James (not the trumpet player of recent times) to play this new lively, syncopated music in his speakeasy called Shillers Cafe on 31st Street in Chicago. From the very first night of the gig, they were a huge success. During their opening performance, a more than moderately intoxicated patron was moved beyond control by this new sound. He jumped on a table and, in syncopation with the music, shouted, "Jass it up". Jass was an underground term with numerous meanings, depending on how it was used. Today its exact meaning is obscure. Harry James, being a great promoter and knowing a good thing when he saw or heard it, responded to the reaction of the audience as they in syncopation shouted, "Jass it up". The next day James had posters printed and distributed.

He also put up a sign advertising the group of musicians as "Stein's Dixie Jass Band". People, being as mischievous as they are, could not resist the temptation to obliterate the letter "J" from the signs and posters. To overcome this dastardly deed, the spelling was changed from Jass to Jasz and then Jaz. The first time the present spelling JAZZ was used was in the New York Times February 2, 1917, and Jazz it has been ever since.

GUMBO

Gumbo, one of Louisiana's truly unique dishes, came about in the following way.

When people of all races are forced from their homelands, or leave on their own, they invariably bring with them a myriad of items to remind them of their roots. African slaves were not afforded that luxury. In almost all cases, they were herded on ships with only the skimpy clothes they wore. One item they were able to carry with them in their Afro hair was the seed of the kingombo (OKRA) plant. Upon arriving in Louisiana, they

planted the seeds, tended the plants, and prepared the yield for themselves and their appreciative masters.

Today, the three most popular varieties of gumbo are: okra,

given to us by the African slaves; filé, which was a contribution of the Choctaw Indians; and seafood, made popular by the Cajuns, who were the leading fishermen in the area.

MONEY-MONNAIE-DINERO

Money is one of those strange commodities that we deal with daily. What makes it strange is, those who have plenty never seem to speak about it; on the other hand, those who have little seem to talk about it regularly, especially the lack of it.

Prior to the Louisiana Purchase, French and Spanish money was used in Louisiana. Both left indelible impressions that are still with us till this day.

The abundance of the unique ten dollar bill led to the term "Dixie". Those bills were produced in the millions by the Citizens Bank in New Orleans prior to the Civil War and were negotiable all over the country.

By 1859, just two years before the Civil War began, New Orleans river trade had peaked at $289,000,000-that was more

money than all U.S. coins in circulation. With this interesting fact, it is easy to understand why so many Dixie bills were printed.

Local money terms that were inspired by the Spanish are as follows:

The symbol of the Spanish peso was:

which in time, evolved to the American dollar sign ($).

Proof of the above is pointed out in the following facts:

In 1779, years before the first U.S. paper money was printed, New Orleanian Oliver Pollock, (Mr. American Revolution as well as the first Dollar-A-Year Man) received two wooden carvings as a gift from his friend, Pere Cyrillo, a Spanish Capuchin monk. One of the carvings was a cross and the other a replica of the present day dollar sign. Pollock, many years later made a gift of these two items to the Ursuline nuns. Both are presently on display in the Ursuline Museum at 2635 State Street in New Orleans.

Another Spanish contribution that references local currency is the term 2 bits—meaning 25 cents.

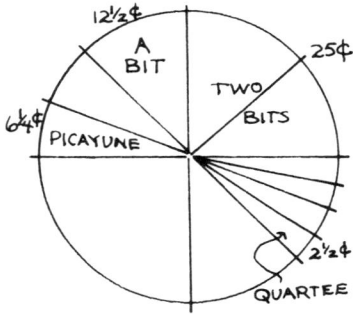

The Spanish peso was used as the trade dollar in Louisiana after Spain took possession in 1762. Since small change was difficult to obtain, the Spanish silver dollar was physically cut into pieces. When cutting the dollar into two parts you had two one-half dollars. When each half was cut in half again you of course had 4 quarters. To make still smaller change, you cut the quarters into equal parts and these were called bits. Each bit represented 12½ cents and was so called because when placed point-to-point it resembled a bitt, as the English speaking called it the "bitt-head", on the foredeck of a boat on which hawsers were made fast.

Note: Even though it is true that the American dime is no longer made of silver, (at one time it was) and because the peso was a silver coin, after many, many generations, Orleanians continue to refer to our American dime as a "silver dime".

Yet another term given to us by the Spanish is the term "picayune". The term was derived from further breakdown of the Spanish peso and was the smallest division of the peso. The definition of picayune as described in the dictionary means "anything of trifling value".

The Picayune newspaper no doubt takes its name because of the small cost of the publication and has nothing (we hope) to do with the true definition of the word.

One term that finally died but was still in use a few decades ago was the term "quartee" (representing one-half of a nickel). A favorite saying in by-gone days when the term was in use is listed below.

A mother, when sending her child to the corner grocery store, advised the child to purchase the ingredients for a complete meal by ordering a quartee of beans, a quartee of rice, and a lagniappe of pickled meat to make it all taste nice.

WORLD'S LARGEST WALTZ QUEEN
MADE QUITE A SCENE

On November 12, 1885, the Dime Museum on Canal Street drew an expected overflow crowd. When the museum passed out handbills advertising what the entertainment would be on that day, tickets were snatched up in record time for the Dime.

Those who paid to get in waited with great anticipation. They were not disappointed in their investment of time or money. Just as the advertisement had promised, the World's Largest Dance Queen was as light as a feather on her feet, even though she weighed in excess of 700 pounds.

Without a doubt, she made a lasting impression on her audience. If, God forbid, she tripped and fell on her partner while dancing, she would certainly leave a lasting impression, or, better yet, depression on him and the dance floor.

NEW ORLEANS' FIRST POLICE SUPERINTENDENT DAVID C. HENNESSEY ASSASSINATED

From 1836 to 1852, New Orleans was truly a divided city. Because of the friction between the Creoles and Americans, the city was divided into three separate municipalities. Each had its own council, recorder, taxing power and police force. Each municipality operated independently of the others. Under this unorthodox system, the Mayor was only a figurehead. The only control he had was over the police departments in each municipality. The Mayor's seal at that time was a crescent and a star; therefore, it was used as the symbol of the police department on the badge of all three districts. The crescent and star badge has been used by the New Orleans Police Department ever since.

On March 13, 1899, the city's first Superintendent of Police, David C. Hennessey, was appointed to the position by Mayor Joseph H. Shakspear. Hennessey was a tireless and fearless worker in his pursuits of stamping out organized crime. In carrying out his duties, he, of course, made many enemies with the lowly element. On the evening of October 15, 1890, at 11:25 p.m., he was gunned down on his way home. Although he was hit by shotgun blasts from many different directions, he was able to draw his pistol and return fire. While he lay prostrate in the street, more bullets were pumped into his body. He was later rushed to the hospital, but all efforts to save him were futile. He died the next day. Nineteen Italians believed to be part of the underworld that operated in New Orleans were tried,

ten for murder and nine for conspiracy. All were acquitted of the crimes but held in jail on other counts. On March 14, 1891, a mob of outraged citizens stormed the jail seeking their own form of justice. They were outraged at the acquittals and took the law into their own hands. Upon entering the jail, they shot nine and hung two of the believed killers of Hennessey. The Italian government was appalled and broke diplomatic relations with the United States government. In time, the United States government paid financial restitution for the eleven Italians murdered even though found innocent by a court of law. Diplomatic relations between the two countries were then resumed. Until this day, the murderers of New Orleans first Superintendent, David C. Hennessey, are still classified as unknown. There are many different theories as to whom the culprits were, but after 100 years, the truth of the assassination is no closer to becoming a reality than when it happened.

After his death, Hennessey's body was displayed in the council chambers of City Hall. The wake was followed by a funeral parade ending in Metairie Cemetery where he was laid to rest. The striking monument is a fitting memorial to the martyred Superintendent of Police. It consists of a massive granite column with a broken shaft covered by a pall. A replica of the Superintendent's belt and club hang from the very top. At the base of the shaft is a replica of the police badge along with the Pelican Seal of Louisiana.

The fitting epitaph on David C. Hennessey's monument reads as follows: "His life was honorable and brave. His fidelity to duty was sealed with his death."

Supt. Henry M. Morris

In 1891, Dexter S. Gaster was sworn in as the city's second Superintendent of Police. In memory of David Hennessey, who gave his life in the line of duty, Gaster wore his police badge upside down (open end of crescent to the top). That tradition was carried on through the tenure of Superintendent Henry M. Morris, who retired from the police force in January of 1985.

WOODEN WATER PIPES

In 1813, the building housing the Quarter's first waterworks was completed. It was located near the French Market on Ursuline and Levee Streets. The brick structure housed a steam pump which was used to pump river water into a system of wooden

(cypress) pipes throughout the city. Benjamin H. B. Latrobe, the building and system designer, unfortunately did not see the completion of his work because he died of yellow fever before the machinery was installed. The completed system operated successfully until 1836, when a larger system was installed.

In the 1970s, over 150 years after the cypress water pipes were installed, workers doing street repairs uncovered some of the pipe. When they were taken out of the ground and cleaned, the pipes were found to be in excellent condition. This is testimony as to why cypress is called "the eternal wood".

BREAD

From the earliest days of Louisiana, people have had a deep appreciation and insatiable craving that ultimately led to the multiple uses of bread. How did this craving for bread ever get started? The answer is simple. Louisiana for its first 85 years was under control of France and Spain, both totally Catholic nations. Bread was looked upon and treated by both the French and Spanish almost like a religious item. It was believed that wasting bread was almost sacrilegious. To keep from wasting it, new ways were found to use all of the bread baked, even when it became stale. Example: when it became stale, the bread was dipped in a container of beaten eggs with various seasonings and then cooked to a delicate brown in a skillet. It was then served on a plate with warm cane syrup and powdered sugar. It was called by the French "pain perdu", which, translated into English, means "lost bread."

If a great deal of bread was left over, another ingenious use was found. It is called bread pudding. There are theoretically as many different ways of fixing this dessert as there are cooks in Louisiana. Of course, the crowning glory of bread pudding is the finger-licking, lip-smacking topping of whiskey sauce.

There is one time that bread is literally thrown out that is considered okay. All who attend the Italians' St. Joseph's Day altar receive small loaves of blessed bread from the altar before leaving. The bread is taken home and safely put away. If a storm appears, it is believed by many Italians that, if you throw some of the blessed bread out of the front door, it will help keep you and your home safe.

A good poorboy sandwich made with crispy French bread, pain perdu, oyster dressing made with French bread, or a delicious serving of bread pudding sounds like better use of our coveted bread than throwing it out the front door for any reason, including one's safety.

WORLDS LARGEST
DRAINAGE PUMPS

When you build a city that is:
1)   Built in an area mostly below sea level and,
2)   Receives an annual rainfall of 58.16 inches, that city had better have a better than average drainage system.

New Orleans is just such a city thanks to New Orleanian Albert Baldwin Wood. Because of this great mechanical engineer, New Orleans can rightfully boast of a superior drainage system with the largest drainage pumps on the face of the earth. Before the turn of the century Mr. Wood designed, built and installed the first of the present twenty-two, 14 foot diameter pumps, (the city currently has a total of 89 drainage pumps of various sizes). These pumps are large enough that when they are opened for repairs, the open end is large enough to drive automobiles and trucks through.

NEW ORLEANS—
NEWEST MAJOR CITY IN
NORTH AMERICA!

Although the city was founded 276 years ago, (1718), New Orleans is truly the newest major city in North America, land-wise, that is. In history, ten thousand years is like a tiny drop of water in a large tub of water, yet, 10,000 years ago, all 365 square miles that are today called the City of New Orleans was the Gulf of Mexico.

When the glaciers in North America melted, a large river was formed; it was called the Mississippi. Over thousands of years, 33 states of the United States and two provinces of Canada deposited their topsoil into the bowels of the river. Century after century, the river snaked back and forth. In all there were 7 different courses chartered where the river flowed

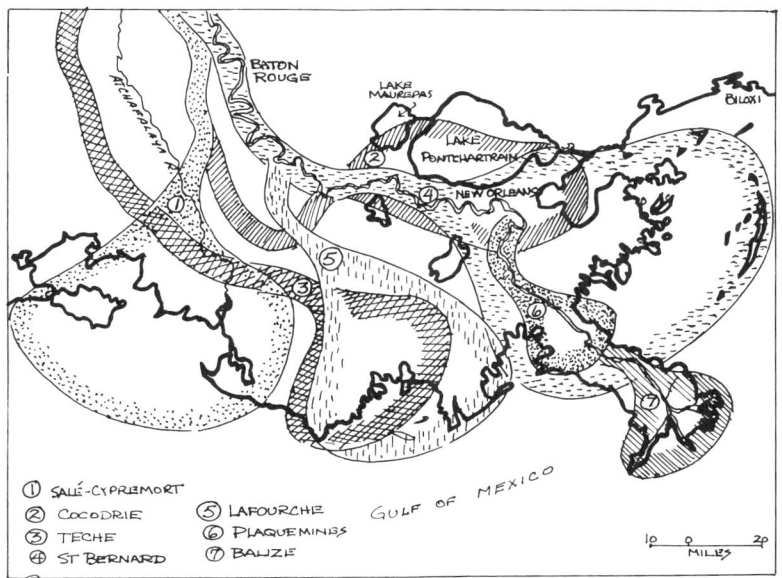

① SALÉ-CYPREMORT
② COCODRIE   ⑤ LAFOURCHE
③ TECHE   ⑥ PLAQUEMINES
④ ST BERNARD   ⑦ BALIZE

before its present location. The topsoil of 33 states and two provinces of Canada were deposited from present-day Pascagoula, Mississippi, to the east, and Vermillion Bay, Louisiana, to the west, building the delta lands of south Louisiana and Mississippi, including the area called New Orleans.

As natives, we can honestly say, and with great pride, we are truly the best of all the rest.

FRENCH MARKET

Even though the marketplace in the Vieux Carre was built by the Spanish in 1791, using Spanish style of architecture, the marketplace is now and has always been called the French Market.

In the late 1700s and early 1800s, the produce, meat and fish stalls were beehives of activity. It was the most popular place in the French Quarter the week prior to Christmas. Because of the large number of shoppers attracted to one small area, dentists

would open shop right in the marketplace. Their method of attracting customers was to hire a band. The band served a dual purpose, one to attract customers, and the second to cover up the painful screaming of the customers who had their teeth worked on or pulled without the aid of anesthetics.

The main attraction, however, was the food. The produce stalls were filled to capacity with colorful fresh fruits and vegetables of every description. People squeezed, thumped, and smelled the items before they bought them, just as they do today. The meat section, with the butchers standing in front of the stalls in their bloodstained white aprons, with knives and

cleavers in hand, was ready to fill the orders for beef, pork, chicken, ducks, turkeys, as well as brains, tongue, tripe, and liver. One unusual delicacy that could be found in baskets with colorful ribbons at every butcher's stall were 6-week-old puppies that were considered by the Creoles as the finest of delicacies.

The fish stall was filled with every conceivable and inconceivable species brought in by the Cajun fishermen. There were selections of trout, catfish, shark, frog, oyster, alligator, shrimp, octopus, and eel, to name just a few. One of the very popular items then, as it is today, was crabs, both soft and hard-shelled. A lady visiting the French Market from the northeast told the Cajun working at the fish stall that she refused to eat crabs because she found out they were boiled alive. The Cajun became indignant. "Mon Dieu," he exclaimed, "how else you gonna keel a crab? You surely can't chop off his head because he ain't got no head, you cannot break his backbone, because a backbone he don't have nowhere. You cannot stab him in the heart and let him bleed to death; cause he ain't got no blood. You cannot shoot him in the brain, because — just like you — he ain't got no brain!" The lady became indignant. "I am too intelligent to eat crabs" she replied. "It's too cruel." "Well" said the Cajun, "why you smack your lips over them there shrimps? Dey was boiled alive too." The lady glared at him and said "You are a barbarian."

"No, mam, not me" replied the Cajun. "I am a Primeaux from Abbeville."

And We Call Them "The Good Old Days"

Walking gas meter installer 1874.

1930s Charity Hospital-two in a bed during the great depression.

1940s-Multitudes of telephone subscribers were still using two and four *party line* service. Today you can call anywhere in the world while behind the wheel of your car, walking in your garden, or in the comfort of your home on your *private* line.

IRISH CHANNEL
THREE CHURCHES
WITHIN A SHADOW OF ONE ANOTHER

New Orleans, in the 1850s, had a most unique grouping of churches. Being built close to one another was not what made them unique. What was, was the fact the Redemptorist fathers built three Catholic churches each to separately serve the Catholic faithful of three different nationalities.

In 1855, St. Alphonsus was built for the Irish. In 1858, the Germans were served by St. Mary Assumption Church. That same year, Notre Dame de Bon Secours was built for the French (this is the only one of the three churches that no longer stands).

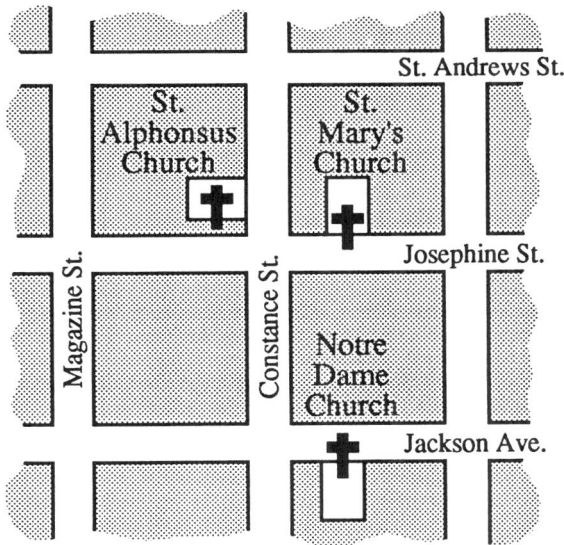

Even though located in the shadows of each other, they each had the necessary ethnic following to fill their pews every Sunday.

This area of the city was without question a highly religious one. In close proximity of the above churches were Episcopal, Protestant and Presbyterian churches, as well as a Jewish synagogue.

NEW ORLEANS
THE WALLED CITY

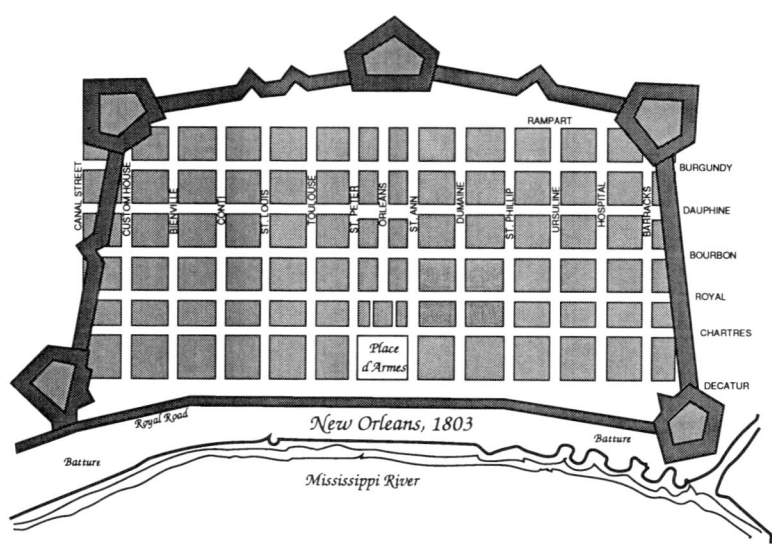

New Orleans, 1803

The French Quarter, shortly after its founding until shortly after the Louisiana Purchase, was a city surrounded by a wall. Originally the wall was only a palisade (high fence of pointed stakes). Later, a more impressive 15-foot high wall of earth, anchored by five forts was built, armed and manned.

As early as May 30, 1725, French engineer Adrien de Pauger's map shows the city surrounded by a wall with small forts. The first written account of the fortifying of the city was in 1729, the year of the Natchez Massacre. In fear the city would be next to be attacked by the Indians, a palisade was erected around the city. It had a moat in front and was flanked by small block houses armed with low-caliber guns. Still it could hardly be dignified by the name of fort. The expected attack never materialized, and the fortification was not used. Little was done after this to keep up what had been hastily built. When French Governor Luis Billouart de Kerlerec took command of Louisiana, he reported to the king that he had restored the fortifications. Spanish Governor Bernardo de Galvez (Louisiana became Spanish in 1762), a young, but brilliant military leader serving in Louisiana during the Americans' fight for their freedom against England, assisted the Americans in their cause. He attacked the British fort in Baton Rouge and drove them from Louisiana. This was the only battle of the Revolutionary War fought on the soil of present-day Louisiana. Prior to doing battle with the English, Galvez evaluated the so-called New Orleans fortifications and considered them somewhat of a joke. He attached little if no value to the meager structures. He decided the money necessary to rebuild them would be better spent building three or four "lanchones" (small river craft) fitted with 18 or 24-caliber cannons in the bow. Having been victorious against the British, he was proven correct in his evaluation of where to best spend the available money. He later wrote that he had sufficient money left to repair the city's fortifications and to add to them. His immense success during his tenure in Louisiana, plus his past achievements, catapulted him to the position of Vice-Reine of Mexico. This was, in terms of power, the position closest to the Spanish throne.

In 1792, Francisco Luis Hector Baron de Carondelet, a Belgian by birth, became the Spanish Governor of Louisiana. In 1793, all hell broke loose in France. Louis XVI, his queen and countless other royal heads rolled from the blade of the guillotine. The French diehards in New Orleans, having never been content under Spanish rule, looked upon this as another chance to gain their freedom. Even though they had tried once before and failed, this did not dampen their enthusiasm. The French citizens in New Orleans once again had their adrenalin flowing. They still considered themselves Frenchmen in heart, language, and nationality. One hundred and fifty of them signed a petition praying for the protection of the New Republic. When they attended the theater they compelled the orchestra to play the revolutionary song. A member of the French Jacobian Society was sent to New Orleans to address those interested in the cause and to distribute pamphlets arousing others to join their French brothers in Europe and Louisiana in seeking liberty. Some of the city's most influential citizens threw themselves heart and soul into the movement. The city was buzzing with excitement. Governor Carondelet, unlike Governor Ulloa, who was run out of Louisiana by French citizens, was not about to let things get out of hand. He went on the attack with the speed of a cobra. The six most prominent leaders were arrested and shipped off to Havana posthaste. They spent 12 months in seclusion in the security of the castle/fortress. While this was being done, Carondelet had 150 citizens sign a pledge to the King of Spain and the actual government of Louisiana. Bands were forbidden to play revolutionary music. The gates of the city were locked, and the militia was mustered and marched in the Square to show a sign of strength. Next, Carondelet decided that he would fortify the city as it had never been before and never has since. Carondelet's day began each morning with his on-hand supervision of the construction work. The fortifications surrounding the city consisted of a 15 foot high wall of mud, with palisades at the top. In front was an eight-foot deep, 40-foot wide moat filled with water. In time, snakes and alligators made the moat their new home. On the corners fronting the river were two forts, St. Louis (Canal Street) and St. Charles (Esplanade Street). They were pentagon in shape, each with a parapet coated with bricks, 18 feet high, armed with a dozen 12 and 18-pounders. Before the center of the city (now Jackson Square) was a great battery which crossed its fire with the forts and commanded the river. The rear was also protected with three forts, Forts Burgundy (Esplanade Street), St. Joseph (Canal Street) and St. Ferdinand (the approximate location of present-day Congo Square). Forts St. Charles and St. Louis each had accommodations for 150 men. They were the most formidable of the forts since they protected the city from the riverside.

Carondelet's efforts paid off. There was no uprising. He built the wall and forts more to impress and keep the French in rather than to repel any trouble from the outside.

In 1796, a French general named Victor Cottof wrote an elaborate and rather amusing description of the city's fortification.

"It cannot be denied that these miniature forts are well kept and trimmed up. But ... they look more like

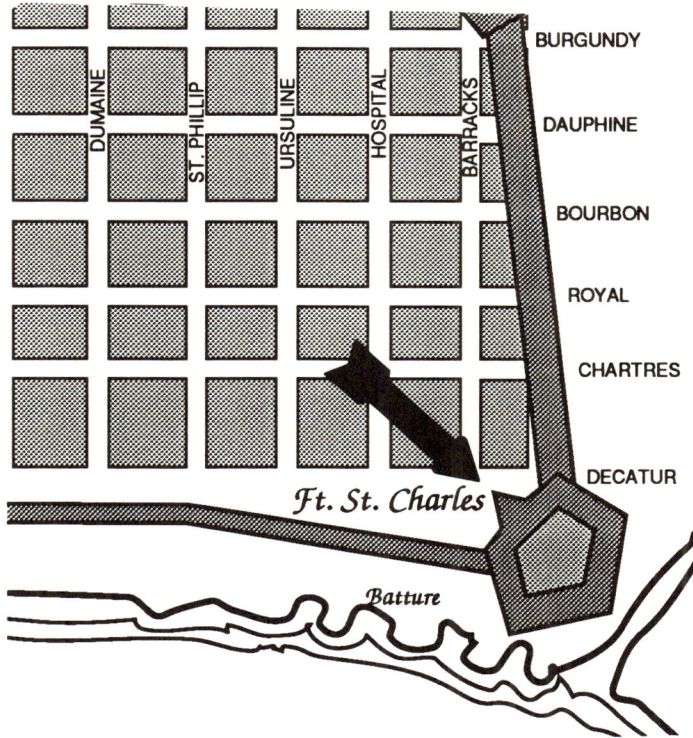

playthings intended for babies than military defenses.
For ... there is not one that five hundred determined
men could not carry, sword in hand. Once master of
one of the principal forts, either St. Louis or St.
Charles, the enemy would have no need of minding the
others, because by bringing the guns to bear on the city,
it would be forced to capitulate immediately, or be
burned up in less than an hour. We believe that M. de
Carondelet, when he adopted this means of defense,
thought more of providing for the obedience of the sub-
jects of his Catholic majesty, than for an attack of a
foreign enemy, and in this point of view he may be said
to have completely succeeded.''

Once again, Carondelet's actions were swift — he had the general thrown into jail.

When Louisiana was purchased by the Americans in 1803, the report sent back to Washington stated that the wall protection around the city was in deplorable condition. The recommendation was made that with the exception of Fort St. Charles it be dismantled and the ground leveled. When Andrew Jackson arrived in the city to defend it against the British, he evaluated the fort as useless, but for unknown reasons decided to have it manned just the same. It is believed it was manned for psychological rather than military reasons. After victory was won, the last remaining fortification, Fort St. Charles, was torn down.

The city's wall and forts built to defend it stood for almost 100 years. During that time they were never used to repel an enemy. To demolish it took little effort since much of the wooden part was stolen for firewood, and the balance was already falling down. Governor William C.C. Claiborne (America's first governor) reported their job of demolition was lessened when one dark night one of the rear forts was stolen in total for firewood.

BRICK
BANQUETTES

In the early days of New Orleans, each square of ground in the French Quarter was called an isle or ile. They were protected from flooding by levees - banks of earth - which surrounded each block. This was then topped with boards. When finished, they looked like the kneelers in church. The French word that describes this is "banquette."

With the frequent rain and constant dampness, the wood did not last very long. Bricks replaced the wood with outstanding results. After the Louisiana Purchase, the City Council adopted an ordinance which listed the specifications concerning "the manner in which Footways or Side Walks shall be executed." Pavements were to be made of "lake bricks" laid in herringbone pattern on a bed of sand. Many different patterns were previously used, but the Council, after thorough study, determined the herringbone pattern was the most durable and practical, as well as the most attractive.

Specifications also required the contractor to level and grade the earth to the approval of the city surveyors and the "Committee of Streets and Landings." After the graded earth was allowed to settle for 20 days, it was to be "rammed down" and a 1/2" thick bed of sand spread over it. Bricks were to be "properly bedded therein in herringbone" and "laid in close

joints." The joints were then to be filled with sand. In 1853 the price for this work for the city was $.69 per square yard.

The specifications writers and the workmanship of the men of the 19th century were phenomenal. 150 years after the banquettes were laid in the Vieux Carre, the Garden District and other uptown areas, many are still in excellent condition, and as beautiful and functional as when they were installed.

New Orleans is possibly the only city in the United States without sidewalks in some areas, but blessed with beautiful herringbone banquettes, some well over 150 years old.

NEW ORLEANS
UNIQUE METHOD OF GIVING DIRECTIONS

The compass terms "north, south, east and west" are virtually foreign to Orleanians. The streets in the city of New

Orleans, as seen in the drawing below, do not run north/south, or east/west as in other cities. Because the streets follow the curve of the river, when travelling Claiborne Avenue, for exam-

ple, one travels north, south, east and west, at one time or another, as he may make his way across the city.

Because of this phenomenon, the citizens of New Orleans many years ago (exact year unknown) devised their own system of giving directions. Using Canal Street as the axis, all land upriver is referred to as Uptown. Property downriver is called Downtown. The area towards the lake is Lakeside. Riverside refers to property in the direction of the river. Going one step further than the compass, natives added the term West Bank. This refers to anything across the river from New Orleans.

This system, although easily understood by the locals, is not foolproof. For example, to get to the West Bank you must travel due east when crossing the Crescent City Connection, formerly the Greater New Orleans bridge. Another oddity lies in the fact that using this system of directions, New Orleans is possibly the only city in the world where the sun rises in the west.

Yes, it is true that New Orleanians are different when it comes to giving directions. It is also a known fact that Orleanians are most cooperative and friendly in this area. Or could it possibly be they just love to tell people where to go?

Next time you have visitors in town you can show them how messed up in directions we are by taking them to the intersection of S. Claiborne and S. Carrollton Avenues. You can bet they will be thoroughly confused, as much so as Orleanians are when they visit cities where directions are given using the points of the compass.

DR. RUDOLPH MATAS

Dr. Will Mayo of the world famous Mayo Clinic was most complimentary in describing Dr. Rudolph Matas. He was quoted as saying, "Dr. Matas was the best doctor the world had produced at that time." At a relatively young age, Matas easily mastered five languages. His appetite for reading was insatiable. He was also blessed with a photographic memory. Once he read a text, years later he could name the author, volume number, page number, even the line the material he was quoting came from.

In 1927, 30-year-old Dr. Alton Ochsner of Madison, Wisconsin, came to New Orleans to apply for the prestigious position of Chairman of the Medical Department at Tulane University, the position Dr. Matas was preparing to relinquish. Ochsner was invited by Dr. Matas to observe an operation he had scheduled during his visit. Dr. Ochsner stated many years later that in his 50 years in the medical profession, he had never witnessed any operation that was as unusual as the one performed by Dr. Matas that day. Dr. Ochsner, after seeing the patient, was befuddled as to how this seemingly impossible operation was to be achieved. The patient was an elderly woman weighing only 90 pounds. The problem, a massive tumor (neurofibroma) was emanating from her back. The operation, as described by Dr. Ochsner, was grotesque, but the procedure to remove the growth was ingenious. To perform the monumental task of removing the massive growth, a block and

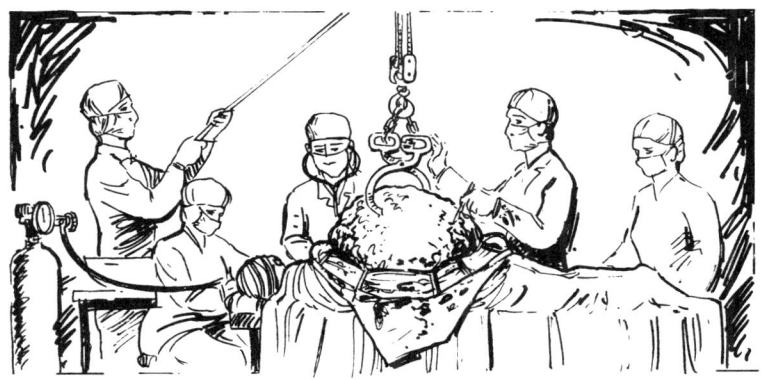

tackle was placed over the operating table. Next a set of steriliz-
ed ice tongs was attached to the end of the tackle line. With the
patient lying on the table, the tumor was exposed and the ice
tongs were attached to it. Very slowly, the tackle lifted the
growth and the tumor was excised at the point it was connected
to the patient's back.

The operation was successful. One reason for the success, in
addition to the doctor's surgical skill, was that the patient

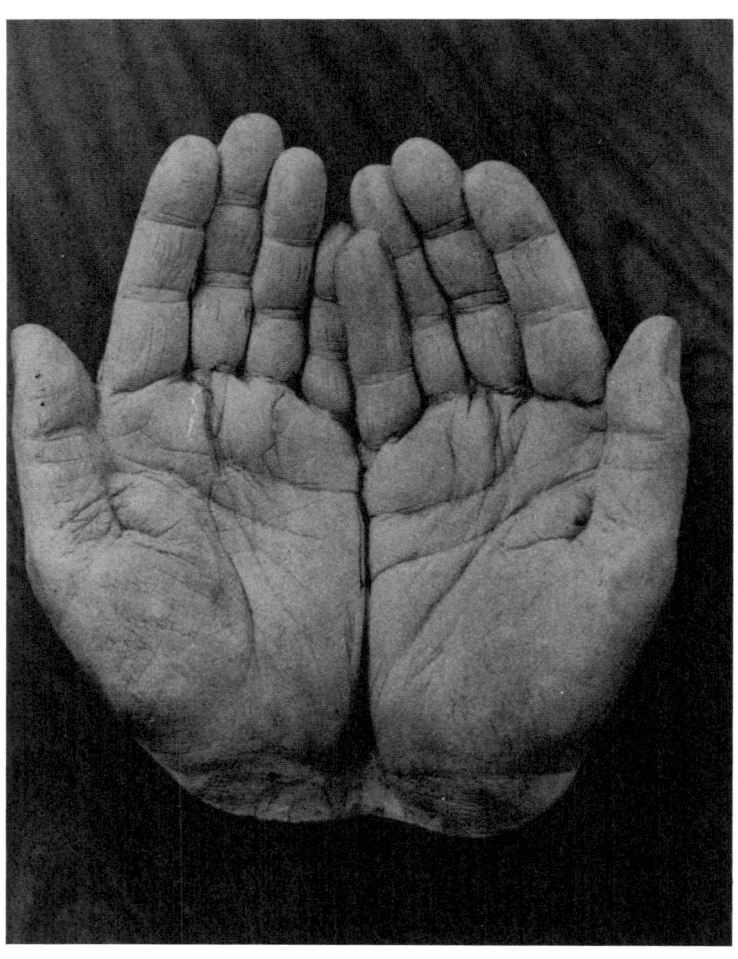

received saline intravenously during the operation. Dr. Matas was the first to ever use that ingenious surgical procedure.

The patient, when placed on the operating table prior to the operation, weighed 182 pounds. After the removal of the tumor, she weighed 90. When the unique operation was completed, the patient left the table in good condition. However, she died later of hypovolemia, because so much blood had been removed when the tumor was surgically detached from the body.

Dr. Ochsner later stated that it was because blood transfusions in 1927 were used infrequently that the patient did not survive. Had a blood transfusion been performed, he thought the patient would have come through with flying colors.

He also stated that, after witnessing the operation, he realized if he did receive the coveted position, which he eventually did, he would be entering the surgical big leagues.

LOWEST SPOT IN NEW ORLEANS

Almost all of the 365 square miles that make up the City of New Orleans are below sea level. The lowest elevation, located in New Orleans East at Bullard Avenue and Lake Forest Boulevard, is eight feet below sea level.

The best way to describe New Orleans to an out-of-town visitor is as follows. Place a soup bowl in a pan of water. Once

this is done, point to the rim of the bowl and give the following explanation. The rim of the bowl represents the levees. The levees are there to keep the city from being inundated by the Mississippi River to the south, Lake Pontchartrain to the north, Lake Borgne to the east and swamps and marshes to the west.

NEW ORLEANS
HOUSE NUMBERING SYSTEM

It is hard to believe, even though New Orleans' population was roughly 250,000 in 1894, there was no standard house-numbering system.

In 1895, the city embarked on its first attempt at having a standardized numbering policy. Prior to that date, when houses were built they were given a number, but the number given proved to be virtually useless when it came time to locate a home owner. In fact, the New Orleans World's Fair Visitor's Guide in 1884 advised visitors that all houses were numbered, but they had little meaning, for there was no organized numbering system in use. Houses next to one another were almost never in numerical sequence. Example: when the first house was

PRIOR TO 1895

built, it was given number 1; the next house, even though many blocks away on the same street, was given number 2; etc.

In 1895, Soards, the directory of the City of New Orleans came into existence, with an explanation as to how the new numbering system would operate (system was only partially complete).

SOARDS' EXPLANATION

"Canal Street and the river are going to be the axis by which all numbers begin. The numbering of the houses begins from Canal Street running north and south. Those running east and west begin from the river. If there is more than one street bearing the same name, the district is placed on the further or more distant street in which such house is located. All streets formerly crossing Canal Street by the same name and numbering both ways from it as Rampart, Claiborne, etc. are now designated and have been renamed. Those below Canal Street as N. Rampart, Claiborne, etc. and above Canal Street as S. Rampart, Claiborne, etc."

NUMBERING SYSTEM

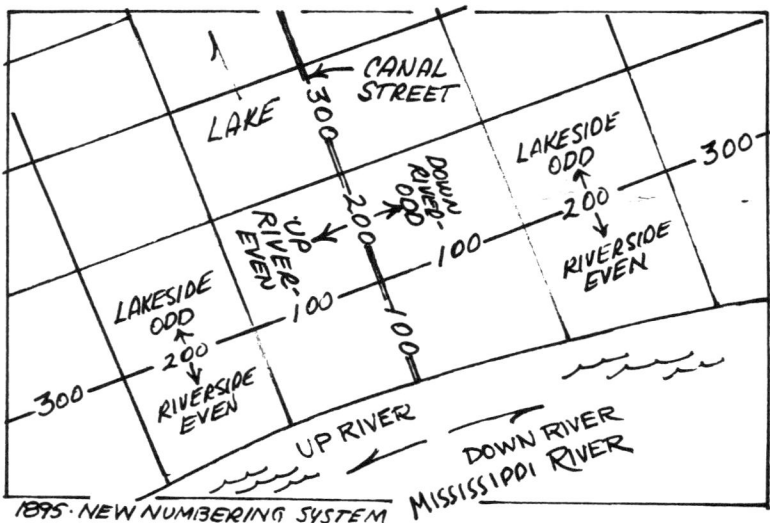

Even numbers are used on the river side of all streets running parallel to the river. Odd numbers are used on the lake side.

Even numbers are to be used on the south, or uptown side, of all streets leading from the river and parallel to Canal Street. Odd numbers are to be used on the north, or downtown side, of similarly located streets.

The street numbers commence at the river on the streets leading from it, while the streets parallel with the river commence numbers at Canal Street. Streets that do not commence at Canal Street or the river commence numbers with the decimal designating the series of blocks at which it begins similar to its next parallel through street.

Virtually all visitors agree New Orleans is a most difficult city to get around, even with a numbering system. This is because New Orleans is located in the crescent of the river. It is unlike other cities that are laid out in neat grids with some streets running north and south and others east and west. In New Orleans, there are many strange configurations for city blocks (see map of downtown area for one of numerous examples).

There is one exception to the numbering system instituted and implemented by Soards. When the City of Carrollton was incorporated into the City of New Orleans, it was necessary to make many concessions. The one thing the City of Carrollton would not budge from in their negotiations was their insistence that South Carrollton Avenue's numbering would remain as was. South Carrollton Avenue is the only street that is numbered in that fashion. The first block of North Carrollton off Canal Street is numbered 100. The first block of South Carrollton off Canal Street is numbered 4700. The next block is numbered 4600. Lo to our poor visitors.

DRIVE-IN THEATERS

The first drive-in theater in the metropolitan New Orleans area started operations May 28, 1940. The drive-in was located on a tract of leased land fronting 500 feet on the east side of

Canal Boulevard just north of Robert E. Lee Boulevard. It covered 250,000 square feet and could accommodate 500 automobiles.

The theater opened at 7:00 p.m. Tuesday, May 28, showing two shows nightly. The first feature was "Golden Boy," starring William Holden and Barbara Stanwyck. Admission was 25 cents for adults and 10 cents for children.

For many years, it was the only drive-in theater in the metropolitan area. The newspaper advertisement identified it simply as the "Drive-In."

The area's second drive-in, located on Jefferson Highway, opened in 1948. As an incentive to get people to come, they offered laundry service to its patrons. Customers would drop off their laundry when they purchased tickets. It was returned to them damp dried upon leaving.

It proved to be very popular. Customers got their least favorite thing accomplished, washing clothes, while they did their favorite thing, enjoying a good movie.

STRANGE SIGHTS

There are many strange sights to be found as you travel through the City of New Orleans. We are not speaking specifically of Bourbon Street, even though it has its share of oddities.

One of the truly strange sights can be seen as you drive over the multitudes of bridges necessary to cross canals that

crisscross the city like a spider web. If you pay close attention, that is, if you are not driving, you will notice that the level of the water in the canal in many instances is above the roofs of buildings adjacent to it.

Another strange sight at certain times of the year can be witnessed as you walk towards the river on Canal Street. When the snows melt in the north and the level of the river is at its

highest, your eyes will bulge, not believing what they see. You are forced to look upward at an ocean-going vessel as it passes.

CANAL STREET—NEUTRAL GROUND

To understand why Canal Street is such a wide street and how the term "neutral ground" came to be, it is necessary to go back in time before the 1803 Louisiana Purchase. Prior to that date, the City of New Orleans had been successfully run by the Creoles of both France and Spain since its inception in 1718. The only real contact the Creoles had with Americans was with the rough-and-tumble men of the river. The Creoles had a favorite term for these Americans: they called them the "alligator men", indicating they had absolutely no fondness or respect for these barbaric beings. The less they had to deal with them, the better.

With this negative impression, it is easy to understand why the Creoles were so disturbed with the Louisiana Purchase. Almost all of their dealings with Americans up to that time had been with these undesirables. As Americans moved into the city after the Purchase, they were not welcomed by the Creoles, and, therefore, moved upriver to start their own community.

Between the two areas, a wide open space was left to separate the two factions; hence, this strip became known as "neutral ground". If either the Americans or the Creoles crossed the strip into the other's territory, they literally took their lives into their own hands.

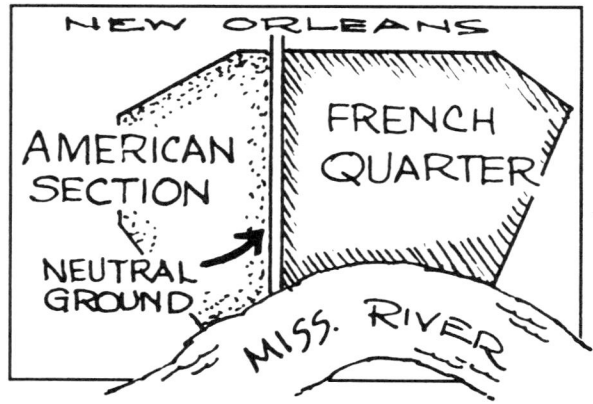

Since they were not allowed to use the Carondelet Canal (located on the Creoles' side of the neutral ground) to get commerce and food in and out of the city, this created a serious problem. Until some years after the Civil War, the mouth of the Mississippi River was closed because of sandbars. The closure lasted for six or seven months of the year; therefore, most products entering the city by way of the Gulf came to the city by way of Lake Borgne, Lake Pontchartrain, Bayou St. John, and finally through the Carondelet Canal, which ended at the edge of the French Quarter (area of Municipal Auditorium today). The end of the Carondelet Canal had a turning basin so that the sailing ships could turn around in order to return to Lake Pontchartrain; hence, the name Basin Street.

The Americans, not having the use of these facilities, approached the Congress of the United States for relief. Louisiana was a territory at the time, not a state. On March 3, 1807, an act of congress was passed, extending the Carondelet Canal down what is now Basin Street to what is now Canal Street, to the river, thereby fulfilling a lifelong dream. At last, the

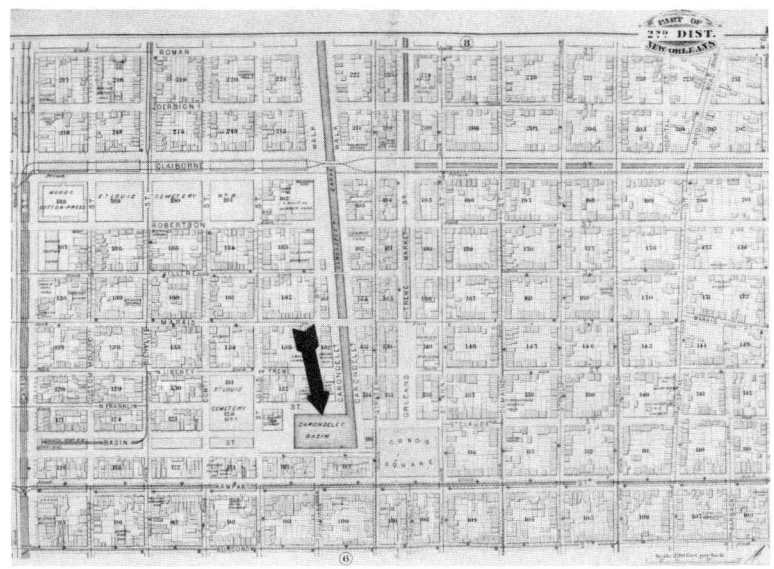

Mississippi River and Lake Pontchartrain would be connected within the City of New Orleans.

The act of congress spelled out that the Canal was to be 50 feet wide. There would be a service road on each side 60 ½ feet wide, making the total width 171 feet.

One problem: Congress advanced $30,000 to an Irish contractor for the digging of the canal; he immediately packed his bags and went to South America and became a plantation owner. Not one single spade of earth was ever turned to begin the proposed waterway.

It is somewhat ironic when you consider that Venice, Italy, with 28 miles of canals, is known world-wide as the "City of Canals". Amsterdam has 50 miles and New Orleans has 87 miles of open canals, but is seldom thought of in the same vein. New Orleans has, besides the 87 miles of canals, the Mississippi River and 85 miles of unseen canals below the surfaces of the streets (many are wide enough for four cars to ride side by side) that people never see. New Orleans is truly the world's city of canals without recognition of that distinction. It also has a street named Canal, without a canal alongside or under it, but only proposed in the distant past.

Because of the animosities between the Americans and the Creoles, French Quarter street names also changed upon reaching Canal Street. As an example, Royal Street in the French Quarter became St. Charles Street on the opposite side of Canal Street. In 1903, City Ordinance –2189 changed it to St. Charles Avenue.

The famous street named Canal is only three and-a-half miles in length. It is born in the fertile womb of Mother Mississippi, and dies at the gates of a cemetery. Because it is the city's main street of commerce, New Orleans is the only major city in North America without a street named Main.

Philanthropist Judah Touro had a massive building facing Canal Street. It occupied an entire block. In 1854, when Judah Touro died, he left $300,000 for the beautification of Canal Street. Since it was such a generous sum, the City Council wanted to show its appreciation for what this man had bequeathed to the city. They did so by renaming Canal Street Touro Avenue. But, Canal Street was so beloved by the citizens

of New Orleans, on May 19, 1855, the City Council met and quietly adopted an ordinance changing the name back to the original Canal Street. For the entire year that the name Touro Avenue was used, not one legal document ever mentioned the name of the street as Touro Avenue.

ICE

It is hard to conceive of a time when there was absolutely no ice in New Orleans to help relieve the heat and humidity or for the preservation of food products. Yet, this commodity was at first a hotly contested and slowly accepted item.

This incident did not dampen the spirits of those aggressive Americans who moved into New Orleans in large numbers after the Louisiana Purchase. They were always looking for another way to make a buck. The next reference regarding this cool subject was in the July 6, 1819 New Orleans newspaper, "L'Ami-des-Lois". Richard Salmon was honored by a grant from the city council to open an ice house. The ice house was to be specifically designed and insulated to store ice brought in by ships from the eastern seaboard.

Salmon said in his advertisements to the 27,000 people in the city that business would be on a cash-and-carry basis. He also had special rates, 50 cents less for monthly subscribers who would receive coupons to redeem ice daily. They were to also receive an ice pail for carrying the product home. As lagniappe, monthly subscribers would receive a cellarette (a case or sideboard for a few bottles of wine or liquor) for storing it in the home.

Salmon went to great expense in his advertising to promote this service, but $5 per month to subscribers must have been a little too steep. He openly complained in his advertisement of July 14th of the people's cool response to his hot offer. Now that ice was plentiful, he also advertised, he would make available another treat, a real delicacy for his customers — ice cream. But perhaps his prices or his open complaint in his advertising were not acceptable to the people of New Orleans. For whatever reason, after July, 1819, the newspaper carried no further reference to Salmon's ice or ice cream adventure either editorially or in the form of advertising.

Newspapers, however, were constantly writing of ships arriving with a certain tonnage of ice. The ship captains took quite a risk with this product because of the delays at the mouth of the river and the strong head currents when going upriver. It was not uncommon to lose 50% of the cargo before reaching New Orleans, even though the ice was covered with sawdust that served as insulation.

A severe example of what could happen was explained in one newspaper article, stating that one ship left Boston on July 7, 1881, with 1,350 tons and arrived in New Orleans September 12th with only 800 pounds on board.

After 1881, very little was written about ships bringing loads of ice to New Orleans, and there was good reason.

In 1868, the Louisiana Ice Company, located at Delachaise Street and the river, went into the business of manufacturing ice commercially. The company was operated by a very aggressive and progressive group of business people.

To show how progressive they were, a few years after going into business, the board of directors, consisted of seven men and five women, a mix that was almost unheard of at that time.

To show the aggressive side, they produced a product superior to the ice taken from the lakes of the east coast and sold it for less. Commercially manufactured ice was clear as crystal, much harder and would last longer. The big plus, the ice was now available year round for the people of New Orleans.

In just two years, a competitor was born, the New Orleans

Ice Company. It was located on Howard Avenue and Constance Street, and the building was very impressive, specially built with three-foot thick walls and heavy cork insulation, with a ceiling that was 80' high.

With competition now on the horizon, the people of New Orleans could afford the ice, now costing $1.75 per hundred pounds. As the old law of supply and demand goes, demand, caused by the 1878 yellow fever epidemic, drove prices up to $3.00 per 100 pounds. This, of course, passed, and by the turn of the century, prices were pretty stable at 25 cents for a hundred pounds, 15 cents for 50 pounds, and 10 cents for 25 pounds.

Meat markets that could not afford large quantities of ice would buy just enough to keep the meat cool during the day. In the evening at closing time, according to a special contract, they brought their meat to the ice house and left it there until the next morning when it was time to open once again.

Home delivery was added as a new wrinkle. The drivers left a quantity of ice determined by the size of the empty bottle left on the front step. If someone was home, delivery was made directly into the icebox.

Just as the steam locomotive replaced the steamboat, and buses displaced streetcars, commercial ice houses began to

Last Home Ice Delivery Service 1946

decline in the late 1930s with the introduction of mechanical refrigeration.

Ironically, a current ice product called "Crazy Cubes" was the stabilizing factor that allowed Pelican Ice (formerly New Orleans Ice Company founded in 1870) to remain in business and hold the title "oldest continuously-operated commercial ice house in North America".

The name of the product might be crazy, but the marketing idea was not.

JAIL
POPULAR PLACE

Over crowding of jails in New Orleans is not a new problem. The "La Gazette" newspaper on May 29, 1823, reported:

"The present jail is calculated for 40 persons and not withstanding it always contains 150 and sometimes as many as 200."

MISSISSIPPI HOTEL!

A new prison was opened in New Orleans on July 12, 1837. The three story $200,000 structure was located on the square bounded by Orleans, Mareis, St. Ann and Treme.

The "Bee" newspaper printed the following report after inspecting the jail:

"Tradition says, according to Frank Boatmer, who heard of it some years ago, that the parish prison, built in 1837, was called humorously, the 'Mississippi Hotel'. This was because so many Mississippians, who came to new Orleans to have a good time found themselves in jail when they could not pay the debts incurred by their splurging. Some owed money to New Orleans merchants and were arrested for debts when they came here."

IMPRISONMENT FOR DEBT

As indicated in the above article, imprisonment for debt was an accepted practice.

On March 6, 1839, the Picayune newspaper had an editorial

denouncing imprisonment for debt stating, "Our prison is crowded with debtors — the majority of them it is fair to presume honest debtors."

The editor stated that he would continue the campaign against the monstrous evil.

By the time of the Civil War, nearly all the constitutions of other states had abolished the imprisonment for debt.

But, strange to say, it was not until January 1, 1961, that imprisonment for debt was abolished legally in Louisiana.

The last suit under the old code was fought as late as 1948.

In the early morning of March 23, 1948, Juan Malamud from Buenos Aires, Argentina, was arrested in his room at the

Roosevelt Hotel and taken to the parish prison where he was confined after the issuance of a writ under Article 209 of the Code of Practice.

He was arrested upon complaint of a firm in New York City that alleged that he was indebted to them for the sum of $10,000 and to get out of jail he had to post a $15,000 bail.

CHICORY

Chicory has been used as a flavor enhancer for a long, long time. It was first mentioned in an Egyptian scroll dating back to 4000 B.C. Since our area is the largest consumer of coffee and chicory in the United States, let's take a look at the history of chicory.

Chicory is a perennial herb native to Europe (the only place in the United States it is grown commercially is Michigan) with Holland and Belgium the major suppliers of chicory to the

world. It grows in the ground and looks much like a very, very large carrot. It has a long taproot and leaves above ground reaching 3 to 5 feet tall. The plant produces a silver dollar size brilliant blue flower which opens only in sunshine. Its leaves are a favorite in salads in many fine restaurants throughout Europe. Its roots, once roasted and ground, are a source of chicory.

History tells us that at Cleopatra's lavish parties, the flavor and delicacies gathered from the four corners of the world were enhanced with rare spices and chicory.

During the ninth century, monks in Holland discovered that the chicory root once ground and roasted made a flavorful addition to their coffee. Voila-the coffee with chicory tradition was born.

Louis XIV was so taken with chicory added to his coffee, he spent $15,000 a year (a small fortune in its day) on coffee and chicory, which he had grown in his own greenhouses at Versailles.

Napoleon enjoyed chicory in his coffee so much that he organized France's entire chicory industry.

With New Orleans being founded by the French and with so many lovers of Napoleon in our city, it is easy to understand why many New Orleanians love their coffee and chicory, and how the custom of chicory with our coffee became so popular.

**Facts And Curiosities About
Coffee And Chicory**

Cappuccino, the Italian coffee specialty, is named after the order of Franciscan friars, the Capuchins, whose robes are the color of coffee.

Bach composed a coffee cantata in 1732 to protest the propaganda campaign against his favorite beverage, coffee. But the musical protest had little effect on Frederick the Great who banned the drink from Germany.

More coffee is consumed in New Orleans than in any other city in this country, and the most favored is a blend of coffee with chicory which outsells regular coffee.

Why Are Americans Such Coffee Lovers?

It was the Boston Tea Party in 1773 which made Americans a nation of coffee lovers. Because of the hated Stamp Act, drinking tea was considered unpatriotic. Traders seized the opportunity and increased shipments of coffee which lowered the price. By the time tea recovered from the boycott some 10 years later, coffee was firmly entrenched across the expanding country.

According to Lafcadio Hearne, one of New Orleans' greatest authors, in his famous cookbook, "Louisiana Cuisine Creole", he referenced cafe brulot diabloique (flaming coffee) in the following way. It is the crowning of a grand dinner, the piece de resistance, the greatest pousse-cafe' of all. He also recommended for full effects and drama at its peak, one must darken the dining room before igniting the brandy to enhance the drama of the flame.

For those who would like to give it a try, the following are the ingredients of cafe brulot diabloique: 6 pieces of lump sugar, 8 whole cloves, 1 one-inch cinnamon stick, 1 cut up lemon peel, 4 jiggers cognac brandy, 4 cups strong, hot coffee with chicory.

Place ingredients except coffee in a chafing dish. Stir until brandy is warm and sugar dissolved. Ignite brandy with match and stir with ladle. As flames dance, ingredients are well blended. After a minute or two, slowly pour in the hot black coffee with chicory. Ladle until the flames die — makes eight demitasse cups.

Art Credits:
Photography and Drawings

References are to page numbers:

Lane Casteix: 16, 17, 18, 20, 22, 24, 26, 28, 31, 37, 40, 41, 42, 43, 47, 48, 49, 51, 52, 53, 57, 58, 61, 63, 67, 71, 76, 77, 80, 81, 84, 87, 89, 106, 115, 116, 120, 124, 141, 197, 199, 200, 201, 202, 203, 204, 205, 206, 207, 212, 215, 216, 217, 220, 221, 222, 227, 228, 230, 232, 234, 235, 236, 238, 239, 243, 244, 245, 246, 247, 248, 249, 250, 251, 252

Wade Ponthier: 149, 151, 153, 155, 157, 159, 161, 163, 165, 167, 169, 171, 173, 175, 177, 179, 181, 183, 185, 187, 189, 191, 192, 193, 231

Buddy Stall: 15, 23, 29, 32, 33, 34, 36, 44, 50, 62, 64, 66, 68, 69, 70, 73, 75, 82, 83, 89, 90, 107, 108, 109, 111, 113, 117, 121, 122, 123, 125, 126, 128, 130, 131, 132, 133, 134, 135, 136, 137, 138, 139, 148, 150, 152, 154, 156, 158, 160, 176, 190, 205, 209, 218, 219, 220, 225, 228, 233

Yvette Ponthier: 22, 97, 99, 100, 101, 103, 105, 112, 114, 118, 213, 240, 241

Martin Marietta: 180

Metairie Cemetery: 210

Henry Morris: 211

Orleans Levee Board: 166, 170

Andy Rogers: 162, 164, 166, 168, 174

Marc Rogers: 172

Merlin Schaeffer: 188

Vic Schiro: 39

Arthur Schott: 186

Rudolph Matas Library Tulane Medical Center: 229

Elbert Vix: 182, 184

Henri Gondolfo: 178

Cover Photo provided by Jim & Mary Ann Metcalf

Other Great Buddy Stall Books Now Available